CW00665953

Advancing Practical Theology

Advancing Practical Theology

Critical Discipleship for Disturbing Times

Eric Stoddart

scm press

© Eric Stoddart, 2014

Published in 2014 by SCM Press
Editorial office
3rd Floor
Invicta House
108–114 Golden Lane,
London EC1Y 0TG

SCM Press is an imprint of Hymns Ancient & Modern Ltd
(a registered charity)
13A Hellesdon Park Road
Norwich NR6 5DR, UK

www.scmpress.co.uk

All rights reserved. No part of this publication may be reproduced,
stored in a retrieval system, or transmitted,
in any form or by any means, electronic, mechanical,
photocopying or otherwise, without the prior permission of
the publisher, SCM Press.

The Author has asserted his right under the Copyright,
Designs and Patents Act, 1988,
to be identified as the Author of this Work.

British Library Cataloguing in Publication data
A catalogue record for this book is available
from the British Library

978 0 334 05191 6

Typeset by Regent Typesetting
Printed and bound by
CPI Group (UK) Ltd, Croydon

For A. R.

Contents

Acknowledgements

This book has its origins in an invitation from John Swinton to give a paper to the postgraduate Practical Theologians in the School of Divinity at the University of Aberdeen in March 2013. I tried out some of the ideas again a few months later in a parallel session paper at the annual conference of the British & Irish Association for Practical Theology (BIAPT) in York. I am grateful to both audiences for their feedback.

I also wish to express my thanks to those who took part in the case study discussions on Scottish Independence. Their pseudonymous participation was conducted under the research ethics protocols of the University of St Andrews (approval reference, DI10486).

I would like also to mark my appreciation of Fr Ian Paton and Mtr Kate Reynolds, whose sacramental and preaching ministries at Old St Paul's Scottish Episcopal Church in Edinburgh continue to sustain and challenge me as a person and as a Practical Theologian. They do not, of course, bear any responsibility for the ideas expressed in this book.

Eric Stoddart
Feast of the Annunciation, 2014

Introduction

It's not a choice. It's more a dawning realization that I'm not like most people. At first it wasn't easy to admit to myself, but it gradually became easier. I had no role models, but I was aware enough that being different wasn't approved of. I'd known for a long time – maybe for as long as I could remember. *They*, I was told, are a threat and, if not contained, will contaminate the weak-willed. Little wonder then that I felt I had to be circumspect, letting only a few trusted friends in on my secret. But, eventually, perhaps I think rather late, I found others like me. I wasn't actually alone. I could, finally, self-identify as a 'Practical Theologian'.

I don't want to claim a conversion – I'm not sure that anyone turns to start being a Practical Theologian. This process is more a coming out, acknowledging a fundamental aspect of how you've been seeing the world for quite some time. There are no guarantees as to how people who know you will react. To some, your admission comes as no surprise. Others are shocked, even feeling betrayed. One or two may be interested in how you do it. Some congratulate you on your courage, while others remonstrate with dire warnings in a well-meaning attempt to get you back to the straight and narrow.

Many Christians were familiar with *Pastoral* Theologians. These men (in the days when God was permitted to only call men to clerical ministry) had a distinctive flair. Their interests in counselling, preaching or liturgy set them apart, but, despite outward appearance, they might or might not have been *Practical* Theologians. The acceptance – up to a point – of *Pastoral* Theologians paved the way for those of us who could no longer suppress our *practical theological* nature.

In trying to introduce the discipline of Practical Theology I am teasing – but only half-joking. Practical Theologians are, I think – to quite an extent – born, not made. At the very least we are shaped in our understanding of how people 'know God'; more specifically, how people know they know God. To put it another way, Practical Theologians are congenitally more comfortable with the notion of two-way rather than one-way streets. Practical Theologians will, to various extents, hold that people's practice is informed, shaped perhaps, by doctrine – or even dictated by it. But, and this is probably the crucial difference, Practical Theologians want to keep asserting that doctrine is informed, shaped and even dictated by practice. No two Practical Theologians will represent that traffic-flow in exactly the same way. Sometimes the street will be one of those set out to allow all traffic in one direction, but only cyclists in the counter-direction. That's all well and good as long as the white lines on the road marking out the seven-eighths width for the main traffic, and the narrow remainder for cyclists, doesn't get rubbed off or lost when the carriageway is resurfaced. Having said that, the life of a Practical Theologian does sometimes feel like cycling against the flow – legally, but with nothing but a faded and intermittent white line marking your right of way.

It's the fact that Practical Theologians swing both ways or, we could say, are bi-directional that sets us out as deviant in many people's eyes. There is great security in a one-way system where doctrine determines practice. But the model of applying theology to our own and others' lives is only safe in theory. It's not actually how doctrine is developed. Real, rather than ideal, life is much more bi-directional than many applied-theology advocates might care to admit. To be honest, I suspect that quite a few people who are very strict on doctrine determining faithful practice will have had moments when they've been bi-curious. They've wondered what doing theology in the opposite direction might be like. Perhaps they've had a go in secret but, quite unnecessarily, felt ashamed of themselves as a result. So, to be bi-directional, to be a Practical Theologian is, in comparison with what others claim as *real* or *proper* theology, a challenge to what's viewed as 'normal'.

To be honest, Practical Theology is imaginary. It is a construct in the minds of its devotees, detractors and now in yours too. This is not quite such an extraordinary or self-defeating claim as it at first might seem to be.

'Practical Theology' is a term used, in no particular order of importance, to identify (a) a field within the broad study of Divinity, (b) networks of similarly minded researchers (both academic and practitioner), (c) membership in learned societies (national, regional and international), (d) various scholarly journals, (e) a range of shelf-marks within library classification systems, (f) methods of generating theological knowledge, (g) forms of reflection upon practice, and (h) topics of interest to biblical and theological researchers. Anyone can claim to be a Practical Theologian – though their assertion might be contested in good scholarly tradition (and perhaps for some less worthy motives of market segmentation in publishing). But no one can step in to deny the use of the label – unlike what would happen if I advertised my services as a lawyer without accreditation by the Law Society or as a doctor without General Medical Council registration.

Benedict Anderson coined the term 'imagined communities' to describe our experience of nationalism. For him, the nation 'is *imagined*, because the members of even the smallest nation will never know most of their fellow members, meet them or even hear of them, yet in the minds of each lives the image of their communion'.[1] I am positively *not* likening Practical Theology to a nation, but Anderson's concept is still helpful. To be an 'imagined community' is to acknowledge that the boundaries, prerequisites of membership, and what is deemed to be held in common are not givens. Rather, the community is constructed and reproduced in our minds and our behaviour.

Imagined communities of Practical Theologians are generated by common interests, membership of associations, or job descriptions across universities and colleges – expressed nationally and regionally. At the same time, 'dual nationality' (to continue Anderson's theme) is widely practised. Christian ethicists can self-identify also as Practical Theologians, depending on the advantages in academic

---

1 Benedict Anderson, *Imagined Communities: New Edition*, London: Verso, 2006 [1983], p. 6.

or church contexts. Similarly some systematic theologians will choose to locate their work within the Practical Theology domain. (The role of publishers in deciding into which section of their catalogue to place an author's new book is, I suspect, not insignificant.) Here we move beyond the 'imagined community' in terms of associational membership and enter the foggy terrain of the discipline itself.

Since Practical Theology is an imagined community (or communities) in terms of both its memberships and methodologies, it is perhaps a bit rich to expect the ordinary person in the pew (or on the beanbag for those of less formal church practice) to have either heard of it or give it much thought. This book aims to redress this situation. My audience is intended to be thoughtful Christian people *and* existing members of the imagined community of Practical Theology. I hope to convince you – whichever category in which you fall (and they're not mutually exclusive I hasten to add) – that Practical Theology has a crucial part to play in Christian discipleship and that this approach to doing theology needs to be realigned with critiques of the economic and cultural forces of Empire.

I begin with an autobiographical account of how I encountered Practical Theology so that you can appreciate the emphases that characterize what can otherwise be rather theoretical discussions of models of reflecting on our practice. So that too much is not left hanging on what we in Scotland might call the shoogly peg of my idiosyncratic story, we turn to a case study of one group of people experimenting with a Practical Theology method to discuss Christian perspectives on Scottish Independence. (The Referendum is to be on 18 September 2014.)

From there we start to get into more detailed consideration of how Practical Theology is vital for what I'm calling critical discipleship. I will show that having critical distance on our world, our practice of faith and even our relationship with Jesus is implied in the Gospels and does not rely solely on sociological or educational insights. Because I believe Practical Theology is integral to discipleship, I will argue that the field needs to be made more accessible to lay people (i.e. non-professional Practical Theologians). This means we look at the concept of professionalization and examine ways that its important values can be retained without making Practical Theology exclusive.

The sort of Practical Theology that is made more accessible is what we turn to next. I take criticisms of the way Liberation Theology's primary concern for people in poverty has dissipated, and what theology must contend with given the reach of a new imperialism in economic, cultural and military power and use these as criteria to assess Practical Theology. My evaluation is focused on a new major publication, *The Wiley-Blackwell Companion to Practical Theology*, which has recently appeared and shows every likelihood of shaping the field in the years to come.

I will aim to persuade you that Practical Theology requires to be made much more radical if it is to serve us in a world that is disturbing and that requires to be disturbed in its reinforced oppression of already marginalized people. Latino-American Miguel A. De La Torre's development of liberative ethics will give us a solid framework to which I will suggest that Practical Theology needs to submit, but remain distinct. The Practical Theology that I am advancing will therefore be well equipped for enabling critical discipleship that is attuned to a world in the disturbing times of global capitalism.

I

Approaching Practical Theology

A scholarly text would normally be chomping at the bit, desperate to launch into a literature review. It might be disguised as a discussion of definitions of, in this case, Practical Theology. I have to admit that the thought of contributing yet another section to all those called 'What is Practical Theology?' fails to inspire me. However, it is incumbent upon me to set out for you what Practical Theology looks like – not least because I'm claiming that it demands to be advanced. Instead of a formal literature review I want to crave your indulgence for an autobiographical account. By telling you how I discovered Practical Theology and realized that I am a Practical Theologian, I hope you can appreciate what it is that I believe needs to be made more accessible, more radical and better attuned to globalized contexts. I know there are dangers in the setting up of an account of the discipline on the scaffolding of my particular experience. On the one hand, it could so easily be hopelessly subjective, limited in its horizon and thus deeply distorted. On the other hand, this way of telling the story might be more interesting and perhaps more authentic to Practical Theology itself. On the third hand, I'm all too aware that my journey is just that – it's *my* journey and, to put it kindly, is likely to be idiosyncratic. To put it more abrasively, I just might be odd.

While there's sufficient residue in me of North-East Scottish Calvinism to make me tip towards the latter explanation – I really am odd – the particularity of my encounter with Practical Theology is a strength. Perhaps you will see glimpses of your own journey or that of others you've supported over the years. Mine is, as is everyone's, a selective story. I'm choosing what to tell you and will not offer you a blow-by-blow account of each year. Lack of space excuses me – and spares you.

In a previous life

When I introduce myself to people and it seems as if they need a bigger canvas on which to place me, I've taken to explaining that 'in a previous life I was a Baptist minister'. I trust that they don't assume I'm talking about reincarnation. But I suppose that if they do, being a reincarnation of a Baptist minister is rather different to having been a Pharaoh or Druid priest. In Scotland, more so than in England, Baptists are theologically conservative, while not a few would be fundamentalists. The congregation in which I was baptized (re-baptized if you will) as a university student was on the up. The young people's fellowship of 18–23-year-olds, having come to charismatic stirrings, was attracting disgruntled Christians from other denominations. Having moved from the Church of Scotland parish church of my childhood to one of expository preaching only a few years before, I made another leap, this time to the Bible-believing Baptists. To cut a slightly short story shorter, I evolved – or perhaps I should say *slid* – into being first pastoral assistant, then associate pastor, in this Baptist congregation. As is my wont, it was *after* a number of years of locally recognized ministry that I applied and was admitted to the list of ministers held by the Baptist Union of Scotland. I retained my ministerial credentials upon leaving that congregation in 1996 to start my PhD studies with the thought that I might, at some time in the future, return to pastoral ministry or take an academic post. When I had almost finished my PhD, I took a post at the now no longer Scottish Churches Open College, an ecumenical venture delivering adult lay theological education around the country, but based in Edinburgh. In due course, in 2004 in fact, I concluded that I would never be a 'good Baptist' again, so I withdrew from the accredited list and from participation in Baptist life and theology.

So, we're talking of a conservative Evangelical with significant charismatic tendencies. Responsible for pastoral care, for some years organizing the house group system and for other years leading the worship band, my context was typical of a city-centre, student-oriented Baptist congregation of the mid-1980s to mid-1990s. We could find out God's will through prayer; a holy life and the parameters within which God might speak were set by the Scriptures. A *surrendered* life was defined in terms of New Testament strictures filtered through various lenses. Colin Urquhart, David Watson, Watchman Nee and A.W. Tozer shaped our spirituality in no small measure through charismatic prayer meetings.[1] Sunday worship was what might be called charismatic-lite with an emphasis on listening to God and being brought close to God in worship. Ours was not the fervour of Pentecostal nor house-church worship – although we did have a dignified dalliance with the Toronto Blessing one Sunday morning. Our musical style would have been recognizable to those owning Graham Kendrick cassette tapes and, latterly, the worship VHS tapes of Don Moen and ilk.[2] Hillsongs were just beginning to influence us in the months prior to my departure from pastoral ministry in the summer of 1996.

This is not the context in which you'd find Practical Theology. Naturally, the church leadership were keen to encourage a practical faith. Pastoral care was emphasized as a corporate responsibility as well as through structured ministries. Yet, this was ministry of consolation and challenge geared around faithful application of God's word in the Bible. Methods of care and strategies of mission had to be consistent with our reading of Scripture, although creativity in the application of the Bible was encouraged.

---

1 The typical books that circulated among us included Colin Urquhart, *When the Spirit Comes*, London: Hodder & Stoughton, 1974, and *My Father Is the Gardener*, London: Hodder & Stoughton, 1977; David Watson, *Discipleship*, London: Hodder & Stoughton, 1981; Watchman Nee, *The Normal Christian Life*, London: Victory Press, 1963, and *A Table in the Wilderness: Daily Meditations from the Ministry of Watchman Nee*, London: Victory Press, 1969; A. W. Tozer, *Knowledge of the Holy*, New York: Harper & Row, 1961.

2 For example, Graham Kendrick, 'Let God Arise', Kingsway Music Ltd, 1984; Don Moen, in *Worship with Don Moen*, Integrity Hosanna Music, 1992.

Now, with this set-up, I can begin to open up my story of encounter with Practical Theology and, more specifically, how I realized that I was really a Practical Theologian by nature. There are two streams of influence – the first arising from pastoral care, the second generated in the politically and theologically charged context of post-Apartheid South Africa.

Christian Listening

We all think we can listen, and often are quite sure we know when we're *not* being listened to. I certainly fitted that description. Having a good few years of pastoral care ministry under my belt, I knew that listening was important but tended to see it as a prelude to gentle intervention or advice-giving. The Acorn Christian Healing Trust was, in the early 1990s, looking to expand their ministry into Scotland. Anne Long had been instrumental in designing a course on listening skills.[3] Openly declaring itself as *not* offering counselling skills, Long and other English tutors had recognized the need for equipping clergy and lay people in the carefully delineated practice of reflective listening.

If I recall correctly, it was Muriel, one of my colleagues on the pastoral team at the Baptist Church, who was first approached to train as a 'listener'. The condition was that she found a buddy with whom she would train alongside and have a partner to practise with and, in due course, deliver training days and longer courses. The initial training week was at St Ninian's Centre in Crieff, Perthshire. While I recall only sketchy details about the teaching sessions, I have a strong recollection of the closing work in a triad. One person was being listened to – not in role-play, but drawing on actual personal experience; a second was the listener and another was the observer. It was not difficult for me as listener to replay, in short chunks, to my colleague so that she could hear what she had said, *in her own words*. I'd found this powerful enough itself when being listened to. However, it was important to maintain the listening discipline when the time came to pray out loud. As an experienced

3 Anne Long, *Listening*, Daybreak, 1990.

pastoral carer I was, so I thought, on home ground. I could pray a non-judgmental prayer based around what someone had shared – that's the easy bit, because it doesn't matter if I get it slightly wrong; God, I presumed, knows what needs to be prayed for anyway.

I don't think I offered a bad prayer, but the observer offered feedback on the session as a whole. Now, I'd prayed often enough in evangelical and charismatic prayer meetings, but never been offered feedback before. It was pointed out to me that I had changed some of the person's words when I had prayed out loud with them. I had done this out of habit, not realizing the power dynamics of offering someone's situation up to God in front of them in *my* words rather than *their* words.

If you are familiar with these spontaneous pastoral prayers, you may recognize the effect. Rarely, if ever, is there an opportunity to correct how you are being prayed for. Sadly, I had denied my colleague the affirmation of knowing she had been truly listened to by praying for her in her own words to God. The moment of feedback from the observer crystallized for me that power of reflective listening and the discipline of not adding my own interpretation to another's words. Being privileged to offer someone back the gift of hearing their own words – in a listening session and, if wished, in prayer – opened up pastoral ministry for me in a fundamentally new way. This hospitality of listening restrained my impulses to rescue. Creating space for another – while not pretending to be offering counselling – was a safe and guarded opportunity, where I could hold back on advice-giving. Granted, it was easy to be obsessional about refusing to offer any advice, but you need to remember the context in which I had previously been offering pastoral care. Whether or not they really wanted it, people felt obliged to ask advice of their minister. Even with the best of intentions, selecting a Bible text to read before a concluding prayer on a pastoral visit was, I could now see, fraught with my agenda. Perhaps most fundamentally, Christian Listener training showed me that the process of being listened to could become spiritually transformative – *without corralling the encounter within biblical texts.* People's insight didn't have to be framed as inevitably distorted – although it would always be partial.

In getting to this insight the ecumenical spirituality of Christian Listening was just as significant for me as the content and training exercises. I, as a conservative evangelical, charismatic Baptist, was lighting candles, encountering icons, being conducted down elementary Ignatian imaginative Bible reading and meditation. Other than the candles and icons, the ambience was not wholly unfamiliar. 'Waiting on God' in lengthy periods of silence was a feature of many of our charismatic prayer meetings. What was different in Christian Listening training sessions was the release from the crushing burden of wondering if I had 'a word from God'. Looking back, I might characterize this as a shift from listening for God to being silent for God. Yet, that continues to imply activity. Silence *with* God is perhaps a better way to express it. The shift for me in pastoral encounters with people was rather different. At a technical level, it was so much harder to listen accurately (replaying someone's own words). However, the theological shift for me was in creating space wherein a person could come to insight. This need not be articulated in charismatic terms as 'hearing from God', but becoming more self-aware; hearing one's own words opened up an opportunity for growth.

Anyone with even a sketchy knowledge of counselling theory will recognize elements of Carl Rogers's unconditional regard or the possibility of insight from within a client.[4] My epiphany within the context of Christian Listening will seem trivial – but the context is all-important. I knew about the evangelical framework of God speaking through Scripture by stirring up recognition in the human heart. The possibility that insight might be generated from a human heart without *conscious* acknowledgement of God's Spirit was another matter altogether. I phrase it this way because the only way the Spirit of God could be 'inside' a person was by invitation through repentance from sin and faith in Christ. I make no claim to this being a nuanced articulation of evangelical conversion theology and the gift of the Spirit to believers. What I hope you can appreciate are the parameters within which we would hope that God

---

4 For example, from an extensive corpus of works, Carl R. Rogers, *On Becoming a Person: A Therapist's View of Psychotherapy*, London: Constable & Co., 1961.

would work. 'The Word' required to be proclaimed – albeit sensitively – and believed if genuine spiritual growth were to be possible. Experience of God was predicated upon conversion, holiness of life and committed seeking of the empowering by the Holy Spirit. Christian Listening was opening horizons for me against which God was less a charismatic Evangelical than I thought. More than this, the charismatic evangelical spirituality into which I had been inducted, and was inducting others, was clearly only one facet – not the pinnacle as my reading material suggested. Still more significantly, my experience of being given feedback on a prayer switched on a light for me. The power of (spiritual) words was much greater than I had hitherto understood and fundamentally more ambiguous than my charismatic theology had contended.

In a nutshell, Christian Listening training began to dismantle my parameters for how God might work in relation to our humanity. This was at once less spiritualized but more hopeful. There was scope for me to encounter God in safe ways beyond charismatic evangelicalism. In fact, my imbibed Baptist charismatic spirituality could be constraining, not least because it failed to acknowledge the power of words; ironic perhaps for a tradition so steeped in preaching and, latterly, 'the prophetic word'. Mine was not an induction into Practical Theology per se at St Ninian's in Crieff. But it was creating space, alerting me to our shaping by words and to a different way of understanding God's engagement with us.

South Africa

If Christian Listening training was opening new horizons for me in terms of spirituality and the power of words, a three-month sabbatical visit to South Africa in 1996 dismantled the remaining vestiges of my implicit trust in Christian claims of knowing God. This trip was, in effect, the final few months of pastoral ministry in the Baptist Church in Aberdeen but, as colleagues kindly put it, 'you've worked for your sabbatical, so even if you're leaving shortly upon your return, you're still entitled to it'. This visit didn't fulfil the clichéd 'turned my life around', but to a large extent it was confirming my suspicions about the too-easy claims to knowledge of God in which I'd been formed in evangelical circles.

After almost 18 years I've revisited the report I wrote on my return – which was based on reflections in a journal that has got buried on a now lost back-up disc. My sabbatical plan was to visit a variety of Protestant churches in South Africa, so that I could be exposed to challenges. Ostensibly I was interested in how many churches were growing, but not far below the surface I was keen to begin to understand how Christians were adapting to the only recently emerging post-Apartheid settlement. In my undergraduate days at the University of Aberdeen I remembered J. B. Torrance, my Systematic Theology professor, regularly reaching into his blue Harris Tweed sports jacket with the announcement, 'I've had a letter from South Africa'. J. B. had been closely involved with Dutch Reformed theologians in the early 1980s, as they opened themselves to critique from the wider Calvinist traditions. The story of a white minister standing up to his Kirk Session one Communion Sunday was grafted into my revising of covenant theology for my exam. This man had spotted a black family at the back of the church. The white, male elders dispensing the communion elements returned to their seats around the Table without having served the bread and wine to the black group. J. B. told this as a crisis moment for the minister who realized that he had to choose fealty to his faith community or integrity in the gospel. At the cost of his continuing in office, the minister picked up the elements and brought them to the family at the back, in full view of the congregation. If you are familiar with Presbyterian Communion services, you will appreciate the double shock. The *minister* rather than an elder served the elements to some members of the congregation but, far more significantly, a white Calvinist minister extended Christ's eucharistic invitation to black Christians *in the company of white Christians.*

As I look back, 30 years on from J. B. Torrance telling that story, I have no difficulty interpreting it as sowing a seed in me about the importance of Practical Theology. The incident was partly an application of theology against the powerful gaze of the white elders seated round that Communion Table. Yet at the same time, the theological bulwark defending Apartheid was crumbling under the pressure of people's experience of one another – at least, it appears so in this incident. The *practice* of interracial communion was, in this particular congregation, challenging the prevailing theological paradigm.

I recount this memory of J. B. Torrance's lecture not simply because I think it played a part in my choosing to go to South Africa about 16 years later. It unsettled me more than I think I realized at the time. J. B. had sown in me the seeds of a profound suspicion of theological claims that negated or degraded others' humanity.

On arriving in South Africa in February 1996 it was soon plain to me that I didn't even know the questions to ask, let alone what answers I might consider. A few days in and an elderly couple at Northfield Methodist Church in Benoni, Johannesburg, welcomed me to their country, as I was standing outside at the close of their Thursday evening Healing Service. The lady made a telling remark, 'We're not all bad people, you know. Some of us are nice.' It's fair to say that her generation of white Christians were demonized; presumed to be complicit in the Apartheid system unless their public profile of protest was conspicuous.

Two buildings encapsulated the dismantling of my theological assumptions. I visited the first construction – to call it a building is inaccurate – on my fourth day in South Africa, Friday, 23 February 1996. I had been taken on a day's tour of the Alexandra Township on the outskirts of Johannesburg. In the late afternoon Lynette, my white guide for the day, introduced me to Jeffrey. We had parked just off the street that ran alongside the hundreds of makeshift shacks and made our way through a narrow passage round a few corners into Jeffrey's hut that he had constructed out of tin sheet, cardboard packaging and scrap wood. The door wouldn't open completely due to the bed blocking it. In one corner was a two-ring electric stove next to a small bench and in another corner a radio-cassette player, a ceramic bowl and a shelf. There was just enough room for Jeffrey and I to sit on the bed, while Lynette and Tseitsi (our local guide) sat opposite with our knees just clearing each other. Jeffrey had taken a spur from the electricity box a few metres away and paid someone (we didn't find out whom) for the power to light a single 25 watt bulb and heat his stove.

Jeffrey had bought this shack for 900 Rand three years before, when he arrived from Petersburg looking for work. Lynette remarked that she had never seen him in anything but clean and ironed shirt and trousers – how he managed that, she couldn't figure out. His day consisted of looking for short-term employment. He had last worked the previous November, but had done short spells since as a voter-educator and voting adjudicator. Jeffrey spent his remaining time doing voluntary work for the peace and reconciliation committee in Alexandria. In his makeshift shack Jeffrey offered me hospitality in the form of a Seven-Up drink.

About two months later I had morning coffee with other South Africans, here within the imposing grandeur of the Faculty of Theology at Stellenbosch. The architecture spoke of nothing but colonial supremacy, and more loudly to me than the warm welcome extended by members of the faculty. The physicality of the building drowned out the commitment to social justice in which its present occupants were actively engaged as theologians in the new South Africa. All I could hear was this edifice underpinning the undemocratic white regime by the theology taught within its walls in the past.

What unsettled me the most was realizing that well-meaning Christian people had had a blind spot. Formed by a racist system and shaped by politicians and preachers, white South African *evangelical, born-again, Bible-believing* Christians were, for so long, unable to appreciate the theological significance of their government's policies. Able to *observe* racial separation and radical inequalities, their capacity to *see* how much this was a perversion of the gospel to which they claimed allegiance was curtailed.

Now, none of us can see our blind spot – that's why we call it a 'blind spot'. For me, the immediately discomfiting thought was – what is the blind spot that I can't see that I have? I started asking myself what sort of faith we can have that enables us to see our blind spots. Conservative evangelical faith, as it had been taught to me, most certainly couldn't offer that reassurance. The approaches to which I'd been exposed in theological education and in pastoral experience did not offer me a framework that could square this circle. Christian faith constructed a different way of observing the world around me; experience had to be subservient to the biblical witness. It was wholly inadequate to simply assert that white South Africans had been misreading the Bible. That is an outsider's viewpoint – even if it were a correct assessment. No, the problem seemed to me to be much more fundamental. White South Africans believed they were being faithful to the Bible – but had got it so wrong.

If I can revisit my feelings from the distance of almost 18 years, I would put it this way (although at the time I was much more conflicted, given the absence of any viable alternative within my knowledge). I felt as if I were on a stage set, and I'd leaned on a wall to discover that it was only part of the scenery as it moved away from me. Christian commitment – in the terms of ultimate truth to be believed and acted upon – was as much, if not more, part of the problem than the solution. I'd like to think that 'the problem' was that of social justice, but at that time, for me, this was but one, admittedly, small component. I'd been formed in a tradition that gave overwhelming significance to matters of personal salvation.

Setting my eternal destiny to one side, I was discovering that the practice of wholehearted Christian discipleship could not make a disciple immune from having a blind spot (or perhaps quite a few blind spots). It would take a PhD (eventually a dissertation called 'Hell: A Practical Theological Inquiry') to introduce me to a theological approach that relied integrally on faithful *critical* exploration.

2

Plunging into Practical Theology

When I left pastoral ministry in July 1996 to begin full-time postgraduate studies at the University of Aberdeen, my original intention was to research listening as a tool for pastoral care. I was intrigued by the middle way that listening seemed to offer – between pastoral advice-giving care at one end and professional counselling at the other end of a spectrum of training. Most of all, I think I was irritated by regular anxieties expressed by people setting out on one of the Christian Listening courses I was helping to teach as, now, one of the Scottish tutors for Acorn Christian Healing. Working almost always with Evangelicals, I was irked by our (or by that stage I might have begun to say 'their'?) sense of responsibility to 'warn about sin' and 'share the gospel' that came into conflict with the much less directive approach to which I and other tutors were introducing them. In essence, I wanted to get to grips with the challenges that reflective listening posed to this understanding of Christian evangelistic responsibilities.

When I'd done my undergraduate divinity degree, also in Aberdeen, back in the late 1970s and early 1980s, Practical Theology was only offered at sub-honours level. It was not until the year after I graduated that honours classes were available. I have wondered if I can get away with blaming the university for my failure to keep on reading in Practical (or in fact any scholarly) Theology once I was in ministry. Surely, they should have left me with the tools – and enthusiasm – for continuing to study, albeit informally, in a disciplined manner and to a sophisticated level. Other candidates to blame could be the congregation to whom I ministered – they had too many pastoral problems that took up my attention, so I didn't have time to keep on reading theological material. There might be the tiniest bit of blame attaching to my alma mater and congregation, but I was too occupied with the moment to consider the longer-term investment in continued study.

So I launched out into postgraduate studies – 14 years after having finished my undergraduate studies – with a paltry background in contemporary practical theological knowledge. I had been reading during those years – but quite functionally. I wasn't even a devotee of particular evangelical theologians – I scavenged for writings, latterly within the non-scholarly, but not too populist, end of the charismatic market. All would have been quite decidedly 'applied theology' – not least because, in my Baptist context, it was vital to be able to offer biblical justification for how we were developing our worship, mission and pastoral care.

I had simply to plunge into pastoral theology in the autumn of 1996 with the vaguest of reading plans.

My descriptions are never innocent

My gut reactions were immediately confirmed by Frank Wright.[1] If his wasn't the first text I read at that time, it was close to being so. No term, and especially not 'pastoral care', is devoid of theological challenges. Embedded within it are assumptions around sin, judgement and confrontation. Looking back from 17 or so years on this is such a stunningly basic realization, but, to be honest, I think it is so fundamental to this discipline. Every practice – within and beyond ministries of Christian caring organized by the Church – can be explored theologically. When I talk to people now about my work in surveillance studies, the most common reaction is puzzlement from Christian people as to how CCTV, customer data management, or their own practices of monitoring their peers through social media, connect in any way with their theological beliefs.[2]

To be fair, some practices bear a few of their theological ingredients on their sleeve (and the messy picture this mixed metaphor

---

1 Frank Wright, *Pastoral Care Revisited*, London: SCM Press, 1996.

2 Eric Stoddart, *Theological Perspectives on a Surveillance Society: Watching and Being Watched*, Aldershot: Ashgate, 2011.

paints is not accidental). Other theological assumptions have been blended so thoroughly that the clues lie, like the worktop of a cake-maker, in the packets, wrappings and plastic boxes strewn around the kitchen. Such a way of looking at practices seemed a big step for me at the time, but it's not really much of an advance on applied theology. It's useful – but only up to a limited point – to be able to reverse engineer a practice so as to identify the theological assump-tions and challenges inherent within it. Understanding a situation partly through interpreting the theological assumptions you bring to this particular practice is an element of Practical Theology. I was quite taken with some early reading of Don Browning who, only much later was I able to appreciate, was deeply influential in the field through his own work and supervision of doctoral students now prominent in the discipline. I liked his idea that Practical The-ology had to:

> have some description of the present situation, some critical theory about the ideal situation, and some understanding of the processes, spiritual forces, and technologies required to get from where we are to the future ideal, no matter how fragmentarily and incompletely that ideal can be realized.[3]

I was not so naïve as to believe that a description was either easy or innocent. My time in South Africa had blown that fantasy well out of the (baptismal) water. It wasn't immediately obvious to me when anyone claimed that they'd 'described a practice'. Practices are not like books that have outer covers or a symphony that starts and finishes or a painting that is contained on a canvas. Practices are always connected to other practices – where one stops and the other begins is not a line on a map. You offer a listening ear to someone, but you also give them a lift home. You engage with that same person in a church committee meeting, and you see each other worshipping on a Sunday morning. Even just those four components make it tricky to describe your 'care' of that person. Multiply that within a congregation in terms of the numbers of

---

3 Don Browning, 'Practical Theology and Political Theology', *Theology Today* 42.1 (1985), p. 20.

people caring and being cared for and the permutations of over-lapping practices such as listening, transport, administration and worship become highly complex. Once you start thinking about other practices such as teaching, hospitality and countless others it's far from obvious what a description of even just your caring for this one person might be in a complete account.

Now of course, no description is ever exhaustive and anthro-pologists depend on making a 'thick description'.[4] What I was coming to realize was that determining how 'thick' to make a description is itself a decision based on prior assumptions about what is important, feasible and desirable. The edges within which I'd attempt to describe listening as a tool for pastoral care (and the frame I'd place around 'pastoral care') could not be innocent. They'd be necessary in order to do any research but the edges would be partly determined by my own biases and interests. So, not just what I could see when I looked at a practice to describe it, but also how I drew a boundary around action to call it 'a practice', were theological decisions. That didn't mean that I was applying theological criteria to the description, but I couldn't pretend to myself that describing wasn't influenced by my theological lenses.

Over 30 years ago in *Peaceable Kingdom*, Stanley Hauerwas was arguing that the ethical task of the Church starts not with the seem-ingly obvious question, 'What should we do?' but 'What is going on?'[5] For Hauerwas, this involved properly appreciating the world as mad and irrational.[6] As a community whose practices offer witness to a counter-cultural vision of what is good, those who are asking 'What is going on?' are interpreting their social context through the lens of a particular idea of what sort of person they ought to be.[7] The researcher who is properly self-reflexive understands who

---

4 Clifford Geertz advanced the idea of 'thick' action requiring a simi-larly 'thick' description; see Clifford Geertz, *The Interpretation of Cultures: Selected Essays*, London: Fontana, 1993 (1973). For a way of deploying this notion, see Don Browning, *A Fundamental Practical Theology: Descriptive and Strategic Proposals*, Minneapolis: Fortress Press, 1996.

5 Stanley Hauerwas, *The Peaceable Kingdom: A Primer in Christian Ethics*, London: SCM Press, 1984, p. 102.

6 Hauerwas, *Peaceable*, p. 102.

7 Hauerwas, *Peaceable*, p. 116.

she is in the light of who she believes she ought to be. In other words, reflexivity is not merely a research methodology, but a way of being that, significantly, is shaped by someone's faith (whatever that might happen to be). This means that even 'just' describing a practice requires appreciating what you believe you ought to be as a good *person* (not simply a proficient researcher). But I don't think this goes quite far enough. There is a difference between the question 'What ought I to be?' and 'Who am I?'[8] Both questions are important, and neither are easy to answer. However, both require to be tackled – probably together.

The questions are interconnected because, as we've seen regarding description in general, what we see and where we place boundaries around 'a practice' are shaped by our assumptions. The same applies to how I interpret the Christian vision of the sort of person I ought to be *and* how I interpret myself. I appreciate that this level of complexity could become like looking in a mirror and seeing yourself in another mirror. An infinite regression with which we are more familiar is when trying on clothes in a shop fitting room we look at ourselves in mirrors in front of us and behind us. I accept that reflexivity could become a black hole, with its immense gravitational pull of self-analysis from which actual practical theological reflection can never escape. Yet what I was barely getting a sniff of back in 1996 is really fundamental to Practical Theology as I've come to understand it.

This is what makes Practical Theology so frustrating. When is a description of a practice ever finished? Well, in a sense it never is, but it has to be brought to a stop when it's good enough. When a student wants me to tell her when her essay is finished, I annoy her by saying – 'Well, you've got to decide when it's good enough.' This is easy for me to say but excruciatingly hard for a perfectionist to reconcile with her targets of achievement.

Back in 1996 I was only getting a hint of just how value-laden any description will inevitably be. While it is truly a frustrating dimension of Practical Theology, it is also one of the discipline's greatest strengths. The importance of reflexivity – articulating what your

---

8 I am indebted here to James B. Nelson, 'Review: "The Moral Context of Pastoral Care" by Don Browning', *Journal of Religion* 60 (1980).

own way of seeing brings to your research – has been highlighted more and more.[9] Practical Theology starts with description – but as a value-laden, not innocent or objective, task. The describing is done by a person; stunningly obvious to state, but immense in its implications if we take that seriously. The action of describing that opening movement, as it were, in the symphony of practical theological inquiry is not merely to excavate theological assumptions but is an act that is itself theological. I want to highlight this claim, because it will be important later in this book when we come to think more specifically about 'critical discipleship' as not a deviation from the gospel, but integral to it. For the moment, the practice of describing is theological, because it attends to the one describing; a person (or persons) made in the image of God. The capacities for self-reflection, for transcending oneself or getting critical distance from oneself, are part of how we know God, and God makes God-self known to us. Self-reflexivity is a tool in research, but it is also a spiritual discipline that is shaped, revised and interpreted within particular ways of understanding God and God's world. Where, then, does this take us?

It brings us to the problem of who tells me who I am? What, in this case, theological voices are shaping my understanding of what it means to be a *human* Practical Theologian?[10]

Who tells me who I am?

It will come as little surprise to readers familiar with conservative evangelicalism in the 1980s and 1990s that a Scottish Baptist pastor would have little exposure to discussions around the ways in which theology is gendered. This was a time before women could be included on the list of ministers accredited by the denomination and, if employed by congregations in anything other than a secretarial or cleaning role, be so only in closely defined caring (but not

---

9 John Swinton and Harriet Mowat, *Practical Theology and Qualitative Research*, London: SCM Press, 2006.

10 Of course, other factors, not least our economic context and status, are critically influential. We will explore this later.

leadership), worship (as in music but not preaching) and children's (rather than adult) ministry. To be fair, my own congregation appointed a woman as a third member of our full-time pastoral team in the early 1990s, but, unlike her two male colleagues, she could in the early days attend but not 'vote' at the all-male pastors' and elders' meetings. Questions around 'women in leadership' circulated frequently, but, in the widespread approach of that time, 'male headship' prevailed – at least on paper if not always in practice.

The notion that the biblical texts and theological traditions are patriarchal was not denied, but embraced in the belief that this was God's revealed way. It was ungodly, atheist women's liberationists – into whose errors ill-advised 'liberal' Christians had fallen – that threatened the stable and God-blessed structure of traditional family life. In my defence, I was supportive of women ministering on equal terms with me – and on grounds I believed to be biblical. Nevertheless, Feminist Theology was an unexplored land not unlike that *terra incognito* label used in late-Victorian atlases. To be honest, the 'land unknown' was in this metaphor barely distinguishable from the medieval cartographers warning 'there be dragons'! My induction into Practical Theology couldn't last long without me encountering feminist arguments that were grounded in the particular dimensions of women's experience of life – bearing and nurturing children, embodiment, a focus on relationships instead of roles, and political, economic, cultural and religious marginalization and oppression. As I was quickly to appreciate, feminist contentions were not merely for equality with men, but were a demand that women's ways of knowing, being and doing were properly recognized.

At this time, and remember that I'm recounting my introduction to Practical Theology in 1996, I had yet to grasp the even more fundamental point that a feminist claim is not to have women's experiences and insights acknowledged by men on men's prevailing terms. Feminists were calling for a change in the game, not mere admission to play alongside men under the existing rules. However, I was becoming aware that if Practical Theology is a discipline concerned with what it means to be human, then feminist dimensions are not to be bolted on, but were fundamentally shifting my definition of human.[11] Having said that, I'm not even sure that 'definition' is really what changed. Under the influence of, among others, Feminist Theologians (some of whom aligned themselves with Practical Theology), I would question the goal of 'defining' and see that as a rather dessicated preoccupation of men concerned to name, and hopefully thereby to control, an object. The search for an ever-refined *definition* of 'human' is futile – at least in comparison with the discovery of what it means to 'act human'; to critique and contend against the suppression of other people's flourishing. Practical Theology is sometimes dismissed as lacking in intellectual rigour, and I wonder if it is our reluctance as Practical Theologians to be obsessed with 'definitions' that accounts for much of others' disdain. Not being able to produce a definitive definition of 'Practical Theology' is only one manifestation of this rebellious streak. Practical Theologians understand power and particularly the power to name. Here we might not be ashamed of some intellectual inheritance from the likes of Michel Foucault.[12] Nevertheless, we don't need Foucault to tell us about the power exerted within pastoral care. Anyone taught the history of Christian pastoral care becomes acutely aware of deeply authoritarian and patriarchal approaches. This, to return to my induction to Practical Theology, was to take front stage, when my research project morphed from Christian Listening to 'the eschatology of pastoral care'.

The end of pastoral care

I've found a note to myself dated 14 August 1997 in which I'm wrestling with the feasibility of my original research question:

---

11 Elaine Graham, *Transforming Practice: Pastoral Theology in an Age of Uncertainty*, London: Mowbray, 1996; Elaine Graham and Margaret Halsey (eds), *Life Cycles: Women and Pastoral Care*, London: SPCK, 1993.

12 Michel Foucault, *Discipline and Punish: The Birth of the Prison*, London: Penguin Books, 1977. Foucault presents a powerful argument for how important it is to appreciate who has the power to name or categorize us as, for example, normal, deviant, pupil, teacher, etc.

Q1. Am I equipped to do research on *listening* at a psychological level?

A1. Not to PhD standard – I have no undergraduate experience/ learning/skills [in psychology].

Q2. Do I still want to study *listening*?

A2. Yes, I still believe it's fundamental to pastoral care, but not generally understood – especially when an emphasis is on proclamation.

Q3. What other perspectives exist?

A3. Eschatological, soteriological, anthropological/philosophical.

Q4. What might the outcome be?

Q4. A discrepancy may occur between theological position and practice of pastoral listening/care = lack of integrity/congruence = stress/confusion = ineffectiveness.

Q6. How does the first year of research fit in?

A6. I established a link between eschatological/soteriology and pastoral care in history – this could be developed ...

It's clear I was having serious doubts about my capacity to do doctoral work that was going to rely on psychological theory in order to answer the research question with which I'd set out the year before. While following through with my reading in feminist pastoral theology,[13] and some of the prominent texts in the field as a whole,[14] I had begun around April of 1997 to explore the historical traditions of pastoral care that seemed most authoritarian, confrontational or otherwise so different from how even conservative Evangelicals were offering care today. I was digging around in discussions of penitential rites in, for example, the Shepherd of Hermas, Tertullian, Gregory the Great and, closer to home (geo-

---

13 For example, Daphne Hampson, *Swallowing a Fishbone?: Feminist Theologians Debate Christianity*, London: SPCK, 1996; Christie Cozad Neuger (ed.), *The Arts of Ministry: Feminist–Womanist Approaches*, Louisville: Westminster John Knox Press, 1996.

14 Alistair V. Campbell, *Rediscovering Pastoral Care*, London: Darton, Longman & Todd, 1981; Henri Nouwen, *The Wounded Healer*, London: Darton, Longman & Todd, 1994; Stephen Pattison, *A Critique of Pastoral Care*, London: SCM Press, 1988, and *Pastoral Care and Liberation Theology*, Cambridge: Cambridge University Press, 1994.

graphically at least), the Irish penitential literature of the sixth to eighth centuries. This from Finnian gives enough of a flavour:

> If anyone has decided on a scandalous deed and plotted in his heart to strike or kill his neighbour, if a cleric he shall do penance for half a year ... but if he is a layman he shall do penance for seven days; since he is a man of this world, his guilt is lighter in this world and his reward less in the world to come.[15]

In a bizarre – but in hindsight not unhelpful – juxtaposition, I was reading the models of care of Finnian, Puritans such as Richard Baxter and the 1980s feminist Nel Noddings.[16] I was becoming convinced that pastoral care could not be interpreted without reference to the prevailing views about the possibilities for humans following death, tied up as that is with wider beliefs about the future that God is believed to hold out for creation. To put it succinctly, heaven and hell impacted on how care was conceived – 'the eschatology of pastoral care' became the focus of my research from that point in late summer 1997 that is captured in the extract from my contemporaneous notes.

Here is not the place to rehearse my research agenda that finally bore fruit in my PhD completed in 2001. Suffice to say that such a broad topic had to be narrowed. I couldn't write about eschatology without getting to grips with the work of Jürgen Moltmann on hope and the future.[17] His profoundly political theology was ramping up my enthusiasm for the Liberation Theology that I had first encountered by way of feminist perspectives. When reading my way into accounts of how belief in hell had been changing over

15 Paenitentiale Vinniani 6–7, in Hugh Connolly, *The Irish Penitentials and Their Significance for the Sacrament of Penance Today*, Blackrock, County Dublin: Four Courts Press, 1995, p. 11.

16 Richard Baxter, *The Reformed Pastor*, London: SCM Press, 1956 [1656]; Nel Noddings, *Caring: A Feminine Approach to Ethics & Moral Education*, Berkeley; London: University of California Press, 1984.

17 For example, Jürgen Moltmann, *Theology of Hope: On the Ground and the Implications of a Christian Eschatology*, London: SCM Press, 1967; *The Crucified God*, London: SCM Press, 1974; *The Trinity and the Kingdom of God*, London: SCM Press, 1981.

quite a few hundred years,[18] I was setting the stage for a dissertation that sought to understand what flexibility can emerge when, to put it crudely, the options are not simply to 'turn or burn'. I could see that my own pastoral experience had in some respects embodied the contradictions – if not the clash – when models of Christian caring and current beliefs in heaven and hell were parting (or actually had parted) company. It had been my intention always to have chapters like 'hell and pastoral care' and 'heaven and pastoral care'. As it turned out, I got stuck in hell and never did make it to heaven.

Rather late in the day it was clear I needed a recognized model of practical theological reflection, so that I could structure what were, towards the end of 1999, interesting but disparate ideas.[19] It was Thomas Groome's model of 'Shared Praxis' that came to my rescue and, as it turned out, to become fundamental not only to my PhD, but to the way I was to develop programmes in adult theological education and, as this book aims to offer, a way of advancing Practical Theology.[20]

Organizing hell

A little over two years into my research I had come to realize that I had heaps of disparate information that were offering some modicum of understanding about how hell-believing Christians handled that doctrine. Yet I was rather like the person disparaged in the joke about their mental acuity: 'he's got the beer cans but lost the plastic thingy that holds them together'. This is a disconcerting stage for a PhD researcher and one that was entirely my own fault.

---

18 Geoffrey Rowell, *Hell and the Victorians*, Oxford: Clarendon Press, 1974; D. P. Walker, *The Decline of Hell: Seventeenth-Century Discussions of Eternal Treatment*, London: Routledge & Kegan Paul, 1964.

19 My supervisor, John Swinton, is in no way responsible for the tardiness in my securing a robust methodology – it was my own fault for getting too diverted into quantitative analysis around that time!

20 Thomas H. Groome, *Sharing Faith: A Comprehensive Approach to Religious Education and Pastoral Ministry: The Way of Shared Praxis*, Eugene, OE: Wipf and Stock, 1998.

I was in desperate need of a way of organizing my material into a coherent argument, built on a recognized structure.

Thomas Groome appeared on my horizon first in his contribution to an edited volume, *Formation and Reflection: The Promise of Practical Theology*.[21] It is worth us taking a small detour via James Whitehead, one of the contributors, because his chapter was to prove significant not in my choice of Groome's method of practical theological reflection, but Whitehead's own manifesto for the discipline encapsulated in the approach I would take for years to come:

> We are continuously being informed and deformed by the cultural forces that surround us; thus the need to clarify and purify this contribution to ministerial reflection and action. Similarly the pole of personal experience is pluriform and ambiguous. On any practical question of our faith life (e.g. sexuality, authority, justice, celebration), we carry with us deposits of convictions and biases, ambitions and apprehensions. Since these contribute so powerfully to any reflection and decision-making process (however unconsciously), it is important to clarify these and bring them into explicit dialogue with hopes and biases that arise more directly from our religious tradition or our cultural life. These components of reflection (the model) are moved by a certain dynamic, or method. The method, to put it most simply, is one of listening, assertion, and decision.[22]

Although Whitehead is focusing on reflection by ministers his point is equally valid for the vast majority of Christians who are not ordained. We must admit to 'deposits of convictions' for they contribute, I would say often more unconsciously than consciously, to how we articulate and practise our faith. It is vital that the dialogue between what we prefer to bracket as 'faith' and 'cultural' influences is made explicit. 'Listening' as the first component of

---

21 Thomas H. Groome, 'Theology on Our Feet: A Revisionist Pedagogy for Healing the Gap between Academia and Ecclesia', in Lewis S. Mudge and James N. Poling (eds), *Formation and Reflection: The Promise of Practical Theology*, Philadelphia: Fortress Press, 1987.

22 James D. Whitehead, 'The Practical Play of Theology', in Mudge and Poling (eds), *Formation and Reflection*, p. 38.

Whitehead's simplified model naturally appealed to me given the road I had travelled to begin my postgraduate studies. Here, listening was not confined to contexts of pastoral support, but Whitehead was reminding me that it was an important skill for reflection upon any aspect of faith as we are living it.

This chimed well with Groome's assertion that would be equally significant for my understanding of Practical Theology. It is worth also quoting him at length:

> The *primary* locus of theology is not academia nor even ecclesia, but human history as it unfolds in the world. Why? Because human history is the locus of God's activity in time and thus always the first source of God's self-disclosure at any time ... Because the world is the arena of God's saving activity, human history must be the primary locus, the point of both departure and arrival for rational discourse about God. This means that the praxis of God in history as it is co-constituted through human praxis is our primary text and context for doing theology. And because the whole created order and the activity that constitute human history are potential disclosures of God to us, then all the human sciences, disciplines of learning, and ways of knowing are potential resources for our theologizing ...[23]

So much of the shift I had made in my theological position, under the influence of first Christian Listening and then my experience in South Africa, were expressed here by Groome. I was affirmed in looking for God beyond the confines of the individual soul and the tightly boundaried evangelical community of faith. Despite knowing that personal salvation was not abstracted from history – I had heard more than enough sermons on the epistle of James asserting that faith without works is dead – Groome's endorsing of 'the world' was profoundly liberating. So, for me at least, the attention of Practical Theology could never be limited to church activities, but had to be first and foremost concerned with 'the praxis of God in history' – and alert to how we are integrally involved as collaborators with God. Although this carried echoes of good Sunday School reminders that 'God has no hands but our

---

23 Groome, 'Theology on Our Feet', p. 61.

hands', Groome's articulation of the locus of Practical (indeed all) Theology was not in terms of us somehow bringing God into the world and, by implication, being the (only) ones to do so. Here was a theology of the world that could conceive of a positive potential; it, and not only the Church and individual souls, could be where God disclosed Godself.

Groome is careful, however, to ensure that we don't make the mistake of so accentuating the present as potentially disclosive of Godself that we ignore the past. This would be to 'forget the universality of God's grace and presence within history, long before we begin to theologize'.[24] This reason alone – apart from other issues around the authority of tradition – demands that part of our reflection process engages us with how those before us have encountered and reflected upon God.

Groome offers, in this 1987 chapter, what he calls, much too self-deprecatingly I think, 'a modest proposal'.[25] He identifies three imperatives. The first focuses attention on what we are actually doing here and now (even if it is action that we take for granted). Next, the deposits of faith in our traditions need to be articulated – but, vitally, we must be alert to hidden voices and conscious that theology (rather like history) tends to be written by the winners in political and social conflicts. Then, and only then, our action (analysed using appropriate social, political, cultural or other theories) and our traditions (considered critically) are brought into conversation to see what each affirms and challenges in the other.[26]

In 1991 Groome offered an extensive discussion and development of his model in his book *Sharing Faith* that can be summarized as follows:

1. Naming/expressing of praxis.
2. Critical reflection on present action.
   a. Critical and social reasoning.
      i. Critical personal reasoning.
      ii. Critical reasoning as social analysis.

---

24 Groome, 'Theology on Our Feet', p. 62.
25 Groome, 'Theology on Our Feet', p. 69.
26 Groome, 'Theology on Our Feet', p. 69.

   b. Analytical and social remembering ...
      i. of one's biography, and
      ii. of society.
   c. Creative and social imagining ...
      i. of the consequences, possibilities and responsibilities of participants' action,
      ii. of the likely consequences of society's praxis.
3. Making the Christian story accessible.
4. 'Conversation' to appropriate the Christian story to participants' stories.
   a. Moving from community faith to participants' lives.
      i. Affirming present praxis.
      ii. Challenging present praxis.
      iii. Called beyond present praxis.
   b. Moving from present praxis to Christian story.
      i. Value in the symbol.
      ii. Problematic in the symbol.
      iii. Reformulation of the symbol.
5. Response.
   a. What to do.
   b. Who to become.[27]

It was this model that enabled me to organize my scattered explorations into an organized thesis. In a nutshell this meant opening with a chapter that named the tension I was trying to understand: how hell-believing Christians negotiated their privileging of their faith in the face of losing loved ones in death whom it would seem were likely to be heading for a lost eternity. A second chapter sought to reflect critically on the cultural ethos that might be shaping people's practice of hell-believing faith. This included focusing

---

27 Based on Groome, *Sharing Faith*, pp. 283–93. For a more detailed and critical write-up of the construction of a degree programme based around Groome's model, see Eric Stoddart, 'Living Theology: A Methodology for Issues-Led Theological Reflection in Higher Education', *British Journal of Theological Education* 14.2 (2004). As this article notes, sadly funding cuts by this college's principal sponsor led to its closure and the very premature cessation of this innovative programme.

particularly on clergy – as the proponents and authorized affirmers of faith. A quantitative survey I had conducted had shown that in Scotland around one-fifth of clergy believed, at that time, in the possibility of eternal torment (physical or mental) in hell for 'the lost'.[28] I was interested in how pre-Enlightenment paradigms seemed to be overlapping with Enlightenment and postmodern ways of thinking. As a way of building up a picture I brought in some aspects of what might be called 'social memory'; here in terms of social deterrence and the Scottish experience of facing preaching that highlighted the exclusionary aspects of the biblical material. Encouraged by Groome's model to engage in some creative imagining – and partly I think as a bit of light relief – this second chapter ended in a shopping mall. There was a logic for moving from examples of 'In Memoriam' classified advertisements in newspapers, past contemporary language of grief in floral tributes, to penal theory to arrive at consumer culture. Hell-believers negotiated this dark and conflicted aspect of faith within wider religious contexts that have rejected hell and non-religious contexts that have their own practices of excluding (not heretics or the 'unsaved', but consumers who do not fit a desired profile for the sanitized mall). Chapter 3 was back on more familiar ground, recounting the Christian traditions of various millennialist readings of Scripture. As a backdrop to texts that talked of exclusion from the kingdom of God, I could return to what had prompted this study in the first place: the change in pastoral care that was no longer predicated on the possibility of eternal loss for the errant or unconverted soul. The penultimate chapter was particularly tricky – as anyone bringing the Christian story and present practice into dialogue usually finds. I ended up with making 'hell' a verb rather than a noun. This meant I could talk about both the positive and negative aspects of having a language of 'no' integral to the Christian message. One of the biggest problems, I concluded, was that of labelling or naming people as 'sinner'. On the positive side, I could see considerable advantages of having an eschatological language by which we could talk about and judge our personal future

---

28 Eric Stoddart, 'Hell in Scotland: A Survey of Where the Nation's Clergy Think Some Might Be Heading', *Contact* 143 (2004).

stories.[29] The terms that had so frequently been associated with people's eternal destination could be recovered as vital reminders that we could lose our future story (our hopes) and be investing in a mistaken future story. To come back to the people with whom the whole exploration started – hell-believing Christians who had lost an 'unsaved' loved one – I found problems around cauterizing or suppressing emotions when their fellow congregants didn't want to hear any challenge to the doctrine of hell. The absence of closure, thinking that your loved one is now and eternally suffering in hell, is, I still think, the principal pastoral issue that hell-believing Christians fail to properly address. Naming this and associated pastoral difficulties brought the thesis to an end with an attempt to outline appropriate responses.

This rather lengthy account of the shape of my thesis, far from being a précis of the arguments, helps, I hope, to show how Groome's model not only provided structure, but forced me to think outside the box that a simple admonition to 'reflect' could stimulate.

While a model like Groome's can offer a framework for practical theological research or formal theological learning in university or college, it is not at all limited to those contexts. There is considerable value in a much more informal use of practical theological reflection – of which, I hasten to remind you, Groome's is merely one. By way of a case study I want now to offer an example of how quickly a group of strangers can bring personal stories – as well as opinions – alongside biblical texts to open out controversial issues. The topic is the impending Referendum on Scottish Independence, and the context is a specially convened discussion group which I guided through a practical theological model one Saturday in November 2013. The aim was not to reach – or identify – decisions on which way to vote the following year. Rather, the focus was on experiencing Practical Theology as a way of unpacking how the participants might go about reading their decision before entering the ballot box ten months ahead.

---

29 I am indebted for the concept of future stories to Andrew D. Lester, *Hope in Pastoral Care and Counseling*, Louisville, KY: Westminster John Knox, 1995.

3

Case Study: Scottish Independence and Christian Perspectives Study Group

Scotland has more giant pandas than Tory MPs. Tian Tian ('Sweetie') and Yang Guang ('Sunshine') arrived at Edinburgh airport on 4 December 2011 from China on a ten-year loan, welcomed by a bagpipe player, the Scottish Secretary (of the UK government, a Liberal Democrat MP), the Deputy First Minister (of the Scottish government; a Scottish Nationalist Party (SNP) MSP), Edinburgh's Lord Provost (a Liberal Democrat councillor) and the Chinese Chargé d'Affaires in London. The photo opportunity of the current Independence Referendum campaign, in a scene from *The Lion King*, would be the SNP First Minister of Scotland, Alex Salmond, raising a panda cub aloft on the rocky crags of Holyrood Park, above the Scottish Parliament building, on the day before people in Scotland go to the polls in September 2014. As of February 2014, Sweetie and Sunshine have not bred successfully, although she has previously given birth to twins by another suitor. Sunshine had the opportunity in spring 2012, but he didn't fulfil his conjugal – and perhaps contractual – obligations. Artificial insemination in April 2013 did result in a pregnancy, but the foetus was lost in late term. With an average gestation period of five months, Edinburgh Zoo has the unusual political decision this spring of possibly offering the nation a potent symbol of new life. With opinion polls suggesting some move towards pro-, might our pandas, in effect, have the casting vote?

Historical context

The prospect of Scotland becoming again a sovereign state excites some and dismays others – both inside and outside the nation.[1] A very brief summary of key dates will be helpful to readers for whom the Scottish national narrative is not at their fingertips. The first ruler to unify the two main groups of people living in Scotland in the mid-ninth century CE (the Picts and the Gaels) was Kenneth MacAlpin (Kenneth I) who reigned from c. 847 to 858. In March 1603 James VI, the son of Mary Queen of Scots, inherited the English throne on the death of Elizabeth I. James thus became VI and I – a naming convention that, controversially for many, was not followed on the accession of the daughter of George VI in 1952 – otherwise we would have Queen Elizabeth I and II (of Scotland and England respectively). (These things rankle; some consider themselves nationalist, but not Nationalists as in pro-Independence.) By the Acts of Union (the plural here is also important for a host of reasons), the parliaments of Scotland and England created Great Britain on 1 May 1707.

There is a tradition in Scotland of Claim of Right to self-determination that weaves its way through from the seventeenth until the twenty-first century.[2] In 1689 the Scottish Parliament was preparing for William of Orange being offered the crown in the Glorious Revolution. In 1842, the General Assembly of the Church of Scotland asserted its independence from the state and the rejection of the claim by Westminster resulted in the Disruption (the division into the Free Church and the continuing Church of Scotland). As part of the campaign for a devolved Scottish Parliament, a Constitutional Convention (of political and civil society) was established in 1989, when a number of individuals signed a Claim of Right. Concerned at the lack of attention to women's representation and issues in the constitutional discus-

---

1 The important distinction here is between nationhood and statehood – they are not coterminous.

2 This list of four key dates is from Doug Gay, *Honey from the Lion: Christianity and the Ethics of Nationalism*, London: SCM Press, 2013, p. 6.

sions, a Woman's Claim of Right was promulgated by activists in 1991.[3]

The cause of Scottish Home Rule is not a recent one, but a referendum on the creation of a devolved parliament in 1979 was lost. It was one of the first acts of the incoming Labour government in Westminster in 1997 to deliver another referendum on devolution that led (74.3 per cent in favour, on a turnout of 60.4 per cent) to the (re-)convening of the Scottish Parliament on 12 May 1999. In October 2012, following the SNP gaining a majority in the Scottish Parliament in May the previous year, the UK and Scottish governments signed the 'Edinburgh Agreement' that enabled the holding of a referendum, set to take place on 18 September 2014. Voters in Scotland will be asked, 'Should Scotland be an independent country?'

The group

I invited a small group to meet to use Groome's model of practical theological reflection to discuss Scottish Independence for a day in November 2013. Other than in one case, I had no idea of the views of the group of five whom I had selected through previous personal contact. They were between their early twenties and early seventies, coming from Scottish Episcopal and Church of Scotland backgrounds. Names have been changed in order to preserve their anonymity. As part of the advance information, I had given them a brief outline of the five steps in Groome's cycle and asked them to bring one, or at most two, biblical texts that could feature during the discussion.

Naming experience

Part 1 was 'Naming What's Happening'. The advance information for the participants had explained that this is where:

---

3 Woman's Claim of Right Group, *A Woman's Claim of Right in Scotland*, Edinburgh: Polygon, 1991.

we offer our perspectives on how we see the Independence debate going, any experiences we have of being in other countries with similar aspirations (or that have secured independence). We're trying to bear in mind what we gain from listening to how others are assessing the situation.

I had intended to take a short break after a brief first session before Part 2, but, significantly, the discussion slipped seamlessly from the goals of Part 1 into those of Part 2:

'Reflecting on What's Happening' in which we start asking ourselves why we see things as we do, what assumptions we have, and what cultural influences might be shaping us.

The initial discussion threaded its way from questioning whether a *debate* as such was really underway in Scotland to acknowledging that everyone in Britain would be affected by the outcome. Some of the group believed that it was proving difficult for people to debate, not least because of 'media propaganda'.

There was quite a concern to differentiate all shades of nationalist sentiment in Scotland from that of other regions that had taken violent routes. The Troubles in Northern Ireland were seen as a salutary warning. Racism and national identity featured prominently, with the group easily understanding ways – although not necessarily sharing identical ones – of balancing the hyphenated identity of Scottish-British-European. Scotland's strong cultural image was obvious to everyone although the sense of a weak border between Scotland and the north of England was acknowledged. The complex economic relationship with London (as almost a city-state) and the southeast of England was aired, but the group kept coming back to Britishness. The Queen's Diamond Jubilee and Britons' sporting achievements at the Olympics had meant a 'very British summer' in 2012. Other emblematic tokens of British identity such as passports and the reputation of the Army emerged. In the final moments before I invited a pause one of the group returned to someone's earlier mention of Trident and the SNP commitment to a nuclear-weapons-free Scotland.

None of the topics were surprising and, in any case, it is not the arguments over Independence that are of most importance to us here. Of more relevance is the process.

Remarkably soon into the discussion people began sharing stories rather than more general observations. Emily told of a person she'd met from the north of England who had said to her 'please vote no', for otherwise it would leave England with a Tory government for ever. Jack talked about his opportunity on a march for Independence to witness groups present from other regions such as Sardinia and Sicily and his conversation with some from Belgium. Jessica described a Referendum discussion she had attended that had expounded different bases on which people made decisions (e.g. utilitarian or existential). She was also willing to describe the racism towards English people that had featured in the part of Scotland where she had grown up. Emily related a story about meeting someone in the USA whose family had come from Poland, and upon arriving for processing at Ellis Island encountered immigration officials unable to pronounce their Polish surnames. These Poles were simply assigned new surnames – in this case beginning Mac. Years later a descendant was able to assert that although he didn't know where he really came from, he heard bagpipes and knew he had Scottish roots.

Harry, who had been brought up in the north of England by a Scottish father and English mother, was quite open about feeling uncomfortable when in the southeast of England, because it is '*so* English'. Jessica also shared a story about her difficulty in selecting images of Scotland to include in a presentation at an international event – she ended up with six slides of Scottish sheep. The stories did not always portray the narrator in the best possible light, but were all the more significant for that reason. What I could observe was a group very quickly offering a degree of vulnerability to one another in the safety of this environment for discussing a potentially confrontational topic. The benefit of the gathering thus far was evident when I invited them to reflect on Parts 1 and 2. I asked them to say how, if at all, they are seeing things differently after having heard others?

Jessica was particularly honest:

I think my sense of, an ongoing challenge ... about boundaries and inclusiveness. You know your observation [turning to
another of the group], is that racist? I think that's something I feel
differently about – I want to think more about. It is an important issue in relation to the English but it's also an important
issue in relation to immigration which we also think in Scotland
we're different about. And it's also an area that I struggle with
in Scotland ... I'm not, I'm not completely comfortable with it.
That for me is something where I feel changed, where I want to
stand back and think more about. (Jessica)

Jack, the one member of the group who was openly and firmly in
the 'yes' camp, was appreciative of the subtleties that had been
expressed:

What's impressive to me about this discussion is the various
nuances. We've all voiced things that relate or may not but
there's a whole lot of nuance that only if we can keep the debate
going in different parts of our lives, different parts of our society,
that could be a very positive thing for Scotland, whatever way the
result comes. (Jack)

Similarly, for Harry, the dichotomies favoured by the press and
campaigners were not adequate descriptions, something that had
been borne out by the morning's conversation:

You can't really make any general statements about any side
because there's nuance and there's 'I agree with this' and 'I
don't agree with that' in all of it. And I think that's one thing
that makes this debate interesting and this conversation so far
enlightening ... it's just too difficult to make sweeping general-
izations [that] there's two types of Scot, [that] there's a yes [pro-]
and a unionist Scot. (Harry)

There were no Damascus Road moments yet – or over the day as
a whole:

I've no idea how I'm going to vote ... So at the moment I'm still in that very open place where [I'll] assimilate what I'm hearing, I'm not sure it's changed anything much really, if there's anything to change ... But I suppose I have a sense that things might change. (Emily)

As perhaps the mark of a good discussion, more questions had arisen:

[This] makes me realize what I do not know ... I've probably been struck with my own ignorance, or arrogance in some way that I'm making decisions based on assumption, and I'm making decisions based on different types of prejudice and different types of perspective. (Charlie)

Bringing in the Bible

After a break we reconvened for Part 3 – 'Bringing in the Christian Story'. The participants' information sheet had alerted them to the process:

we've consciously held back on that in the first couple of stages. Now we bring the passages of Scripture that we think bear upon the Scottish Independence Debate. There isn't a set text for us to consider – we each bring a passage (or two).

I was hoping that, by me not setting a text and by introducing the Bible only at this stage, the group would feel free to respond as readers – not as exegetes of authors' possible intentions. The choices were not anything I anticipated: Jacob wrestling with the angel at the Jabbok ford, Paul's injunctions to the Christians of Rome to obey the civil authorities, to the Colossians to let Christ's peace rule in their hearts, to Timothy against fear, and to the Corinthian church to recognize one another as members of the body of Christ, and Haggai's prophetic declaration of shaken heavens and earth.

Wrestling at Jabbok ford

> The same night he got up and took his two wives, his two maids, and his eleven children, and crossed the ford of the Jabbok ... Jacob was left alone; and a man wrestled with him until daybreak ... Jacob called the place Peniel, saying, 'For I have seen God face to face, and yet my life is preserved.' The sun rose upon him as he passed Peniel, limping because of his hip. Therefore to this day the Israelites do not eat the thigh muscle that is on the hip socket, because he struck Jacob on the hip socket at the thigh muscle. (Gen. 32.22–32, NRSV)

For Jack this carried overtones of community, and a people with a new name; the 'struggle in the darkness' takes place on 'the verge of a new future'. It seemed to me that the rest of the group weren't quite sure what to make of Jack's contribution, because there was quite a lengthy silence before anyone responded. Harry could partly identify with the motif of wrestling, but the idea of a new name for that spot (Peniel) was a sticking point for him. Yet he conceded that limping away injured and what this meant for future Israelite food rules might stir associations with the generational impact of the Referendum decision.

Jessica could see perhaps a change of name was going to happen – regardless of the outcome of the vote – because Scotland will mean something different to those beyond her borders once a decision has been made. Charlie, on the other hand, was not comfortable with reinforcing what he perceived to be common Christian rhetoric – at least in the circles in which he moved – that the new is always better.

Submitting to God's instituted authorities

Emily had already expressed her difficulty in identifying a passage to bring to the group because, as she said, 'theologically I'm struggling to find permission for [this]'. She did, however, opt for two passages about citizenship – Christians' responsibilities to civil authorities (Rom. 13.1–7) and Christians' citizenship in heaven:

Let every person be subject to the governing authorities; for there is no authority except from God, and those authorities that exist have been instituted by God. Therefore whoever resists authority resists what God has appointed, and those who resist will incur judgement. (Rom. 13.1–2, NRSV)

For here we have no lasting city, but we are looking for the city that is to come. (Heb. 13.14, NRSV)

Emily was able to explain her own pondering that if we are under the government in Westminster we should be submissive to it. Others quickly pointed out that living in Scotland meant being under authority for a number of major factors, such as health and education, to the parliament here. The conjunction of the two passages she had chosen was important for Emily because, from a theological standpoint, she is 'not a citizen of the UK but of the kingdom of God'. This didn't go unchallenged. Jessica wanted to affirm that everything is God's. Harry acknowledged his actions in civil disobedience when protesting against nuclear weapons. Two competing authorities are in play for him, and Emily herself raised the classic question of Christians in Nazi Germany.

Harry voiced the possibility of 'reading Paul in the light of Paul' in which the Apostle's own experience of disobeying rulers by preaching is 'leaving space for disagreement'. As much as the group could see different ways of interpreting these texts, Harry saw a danger of 'trying to sanitize' or take control of it. Having heard the others engage with her text, Emily felt it 'becomes less oppressive' and the discussion 'gives me more permission to wrestle with it'.

Shaking and tears

Charlie's is a particularly interesting stance given his self-questioning of '[h]ow relevant I really think the Bible is to this political discussion. Scripture ends up clouding the matter.' It was more complicated still for Charlie because he asks the obvious but rarely voiced question as to whether 'in democratic society God is rigging the votes'. Still 'more worryingly' for him is pondering '[w]hen does Scripture stop us from acting in a way that mak[es] any change'; if when it might 'curb any sense of action'. Making our reading of the text wholly individual was problematic too: 'if just coming from me in what sense is that Christian?'

Nevertheless, while admitting that he had found the exercise 'so contrived to me ... and then it wasn't so kind of contrived', Charlie offered a passage from Haggai:

> For thus says the LORD of hosts: Once again, in a little while, I will shake the heavens and the earth and the sea and the dry land; and I will shake all the nations, so that the treasure of all nations shall come, and I will fill this house with splendour, says the LORD of hosts. The silver is mine, and the gold is mine, says the LORD of hosts. The latter splendour of this house shall be greater than the former, says the LORD of hosts; and in this place I will give prosperity, says the LORD of hosts. (Haggai 2.6–9, NRSV)

The shaking and things out of control captures for Charlie the uncertain period we are in prior to the vote. He was adamant that he was not choosing this text to suggest that the new house would be better than the former house. For him, a second text was crucial:

> for the Lamb at the centre of the throne will be their shepherd, and he will guide them to springs of the water of life, and God will wipe away every tear from their eyes. (Rev. 7.17, NRSV)

Human action might echo this eschatological hope by the wiping away of tears. If an independent Scotland is needed for that objective to be achieved, then he needs to be on board he said; if not, he'd resist it.

Jack noted that this was the only portion of Haggai he knew, because it appears in Handel's *Messiah* – a piece written by a German during a time of 'butchering of the Scots'. The group chose not to follow up this allusion.[4] Instead, the Haggai and Revelation texts

---

4 Jack referred to this being 'post-Culloden', but had his dates awry. For a discussion of the Jacobite cause and its rebellions against the British

took them into discussing the concept of 'better', as it circulates in the Independence debate. Here, perhaps more than elsewhere in the day, there was an edge to the discussion. Emily wanted to again set the wider context – 'will England be worse off?' she asked. Jack didn't want the 'better' claim to be mis-assigned to the 'yes' campaign for the argument is, for him, one of bringing responsibility closer to home – 'if it's worse, then it's our responsibility'. The group churned around the possibilities of voting patterns in England without Scotland – assuming a Tory-dominated southeast that outvotes the remainder of England.

Jessica suggested that Scotland retaining a public sector that helps vulnerable people and without such high disparity in wealth might inspire English voters that things could be different for them too. The difference in the group seemed to be based around the authenticity of 'representation' in a democratic process that returns a Tory government with such little support in Scotland. Closely related to this, Harry believed Labour's 'No' campaign was tainted by the obvious advantage for them in retaining Scotland in the UK as their heartland support straddles the border.[5]

Reflecting on what he had heard from others' responses to his chosen texts, Charlie noted that people were seeing Scotland and England as particular houses rather than currently one house: 'Not sure how I feel about that.'

One but different

Harry presented his text:

> For just as the body is one and has many members, and all the members of the body, though many, are one body, so it is with Christ … If one member suffers, all suffer together with it; if one

---

Protestant state in 1715 and 1745, see T. M. Devine, *The Scottish Nation 1700–2000*, London: Penguin Books, 1999, pp. 31–48. The worst of the retribution by the government followed the rebels' defeat at Culloden in 1746, five years after Handel had completed his oratorio.

5 There are 'rebel' Labour Party members who support Scottish Independence.

member is honoured, all rejoice together with it. (1 Cor. 12.12, 26, NRSV)

He immediately acknowledged that such a principle could be expanded to include the European Union and clarified that he was *not* alluding to the 1707 Union of the Scottish and English parliaments as the body of Christ!

For Emily it was more a text about difference and being allowed to function in our various ways so the question became one of whether Scotland is being allowed to operate in its own way. She posed the possibility that Scotland could be considered the conscience of the UK. The desirability of a written constitution then surfaced, but the effects of corporate influence on even constitutional countries was observed – specifically vis-à-vis the alleged overriding of local opinion that was against the granting for planning permission to Donald Trump's golf course and hotel complex in northeast Scotland, within the First Minister's constituency of Aberdeenshire East. This took the group into the problem of personality politics (particularly around UK Prime Minister David Cameron and Scotland's First Minister, Alex Salmond) and what that might mean for the Referendum decision.

Fear and peace

Jessica's offering was by allusion rather than direct reference to texts. She wanted to connect a 'spirit of fear' with what people in Scotland are facing: 'just change in huge institutions' and 'trusting to find the resources in a time of recession to do all the work that's needing to be done'. In the context of 'such unknowns' without continuity with the past: 'This is *new.*' Emily liked the idea of 'following the peace' as a way of making a decision and Charlie was aware that fear was, for him, 'clouding a more rigorous examination of the facts'.[6] This took the group into speculations and accusations

---

6 Charlie was speaking of occasions when he had encouraged others, on issues of change, and it is possible that he was including more than himself in his comment about the clouding effects of fear.

abroad that the 'Better Together' campaign had a communications strategy called 'Project Fear'. It seemed to Harry that at least the fear of questioning the political setting had been overcome. 'The Union is not a sort of sacred cow', and, as he so pithily put it, 'the Union is not in Genesis 1'.

After a short silent pause I invited the group to reflect on where they were – having done both Parts 3 and 4 of the process. They had slid from Part 3 into Part 4, which the information sheet had described as:

> Our stories and the Christian stories in which we talk about what the previous weeks have affirmed and/or challenged in our approach to the topic. Where might the Scriptures challenge the notion of 'Scottish'; where might the political, cultural, social, economic or any other dimensions of Independence challenge the way we have been reading the biblical texts?

Charlie was first to speak, seeing the purpose of Independence in social justice terms:

> I think what's been interesting for me has maybe been seeing the values and aspirations separate from [in] some ways the outcome from this Referendum. Some of the values – education is a priority, health is a priority – and actually realizing that those are the things I'm going to gravitate towards – so [the] question is now what is the best way to get there, to get those values ... (Charlie)

The emotional impact of reflecting on the upcoming decision was uppermost for Jessica:

> Taking time in quietness to let ... I found myself getting quite upset, and I think it's recalling conversations with the guy who looks after the grounds ... where I work and sort of lowest grade of payment people, and they're all for; they're all going to vote no. And me telling you about that place where it was really difficult for me to discuss with people who educationally would be my peers ... (Jessica)

For Harry, who admitted to finding discussing the Bible the most difficult step, it was the recurring of particular themes that struck him most:

> we have sat for several hours, and we have covered a lot ... [and had] a real recognition of the complexity but not travelled that far; but we have – [I'm] struggling to put it into words ... we have travelled a long way, but it keeps coming back to the first issues we raised. Maybe that's highlighting the fact that they are the biggest key issues ... (Harry)

Emily was finding clarity by this point in the day, not, it appears, yet in *how* she would vote, but on the grounds on which she'd make that decision in September:

> For me it's clarified the criteria that I will use to make my decision. And that's really helpful, because I had no idea, no idea where to begin. I was floundering around in a mass of information or non-information from both sides of the debate or the argument. And just always thinking how do I approach this from a theological or scriptural perspective. So it's been really helpful to me.

Jack, the already-convinced Independence voter, had a different take on where the discussions had brought him:

> It underlines how I am ready for the White Paper and look forward to it ... which will give us hopefully some clarity or more clarity – because I think Nicola Sturgeon is very good at giving information out and arguing ... the White Paper will hopefully be a manifesto for what Independence means for the Nationalists in government ... and maybe other parties will come up with other manifestos. (Jack)

Responding

The fifth step in the cycle was circumscribed in advance in order that no one in the group felt under any pressure to either reach a conclusion or to divulge their voting intention:

> 'How do we respond?' not in terms of how we will each vote in the Referendum but pondering together what sort of responses we might need to make personally, in association with others and perhaps at a broader political level too.

As might be expected from the direction of the conversation, participants used phrases such as 'the leap of faith' and 'even knowing what we don't know' regarding the more information they felt they would need. (The exigencies of writing this book and the imminent Christmas holiday period meant that the group needed to meet before the publication of the Scottish government's White Paper on 26 November 2013.)

Jessica made perhaps the most telling remark about her anxiety over attending Referendum events that would be clearly under the auspices of the 'Yes' campaign. She drew comparisons with the challenge of it being 'like saying you're a Christian or something'. Jessica's further comments about 'the smaller things' perhaps being important, such as university opportunities for Scottish students at Oxbridge, seemed to hit a nerve. These became questions of privilege – rehearsed in Edinburgh through the frequency with which some people are asked about the school they attended – and holding intellectual rigour without its baggage. The 'fear' word also kept coming back about 'the little things' and the prospect of disagreement.

The process

After another brief pause the group were invited to make any observations about the process they'd been through during the day. There was at least one potential 'convert' to the value of Practical Theology – at least as part of what is needed among Christians.

Charlie, who has both undergraduate and postgraduate degrees in theology, was very open:

> When I received the information I thought this is so typical Practical Theology! Where's the substance in this? If I'm being honest. Where's the detail? Oh, this is just everything I hate about Practical Theology. And I actually found it very helpful and very positive [*laughter*] … What I want is I want the experts in, tell me what … I want to take the information in, analyse and process it. Maybe that's another [aspect]. Looking at this I'm not going to get anywhere with this … it was really helpful, beneficial as a part of a bigger picture; perhaps it's not everything obviously but [it] has a very important role, certainly in the life of the Church. (Charlie)

Charlie had not been alone in his reticence, but Jack's suspicion had been around the connection to an academic discipline:

> I also, like Charlie, had some misgivings … [about this] as an academic process and you've made very similar remarks about how you were hoping about Practical Theology. I think of myself as a Practical Theologian all my life; I've never done any other kind; I've given up on reading theology years ago, you know … But this has been a really helpful experience of [Practical Theology]. And there are so many offshoots of what we've been discussing that we can follow up. (Jack)

Harry reflected on his undergraduate encounters with Practical Theology too:

> I think I came with the scepticism of Practical Theology – where does that come from? … I have this integral scepticism, where's the substance, it's all 'just write nice things and [they'll] pass you' which isn't true and something like this proves that Practical Theology has substance and depth and has a strong mechanism of guiding … and there's not been this need to steer it one way or another, just to allow it to play out has been good; [shows]

how well-guided conversation can be beneficial. Not necessarily to bring [you] to firm conclusions [and] not necessarily be the whole picture but it's certainly a powerful tool in guiding people through their own thinking as well as hearing others. (Harry)

Jessica's initial ambivalence about a process such as this had stemmed from rather different experiences:

I think it can be difficult when Christians come together and share; and share Bible passages and look at things ... [I think] 'this is trite, get me out of here'. I have had that [feeling] – and I haven't at all felt that [here]. So I would say that [keep] whatever in the process ... enables sticking with it and trying to listen and taking risks and trying to hear. And to [know] that in one's life one's got to go away and try and understand this more ... I feel that people have stayed with it and spoken out from their experience rather than some interpretation of the scripture. (Jessica)

Harry came back in again to focus specifically on his fears for the biblical step in the cycle:

I was worried when I knew that you wanted us to bring a passage of scripture, and I think it was the worry that you [Jessica] sort of raised that here we are and we're going to have God used as a tool to force the agenda or ... here's time for some really bad exegesis where [*laughter*] we show how this passage is really about this. But actually it was interesting to watch today how I think we approached that section with that slight air of scepticism and slight worry. But actually how it did illuminate our conversation and was actually an interesting guide into some areas that I don't think we would have touched on if we hadn't come from those stories and those passages ... (Harry)

This prompted Jessica to clarify and expand on her earlier comment:

and the word that was in my head was ... and I did use the word 'trite' and I wondered if I should, and I found there was a treat

– you know what I mean? – I felt that they were nurturing and really helpful. (Jessica)

Harry offered a summary of Jessica's and his own concerns: 'hermeneutics with a crow-bar'. The possibility of engagement with the biblical texts had clearly unearthed some significant concerns about this step. Charlie went back to his earlier contribution and opened up a discussion about the authority of the Bible:

I do wonder with the scripture section, it was oddly ... it felt quite natural for something like that, I was worried that it would feel arbitrary and contrived. I wonder whether there's something unique about the text that helped us or whether it's a text that we all are, in some regard, familiar with because of attending church. But actually, if we went to a book group and we were all really familiar with *Great Expectations*, could we have used that equally ...? (Charlie)

Emily had been particularly exercised over the importance of a passage such as that from Romans about submission to the civil authorities:

something about the authority of the text? That we actually believe that this has an authority so it wouldn't be the same with *Great Expectations* – *Great Expectations* might illuminate our thinking, but we wouldn't expect *Great Expectations* to guide our behaviour. (Emily)

This topic was the only point in the day when someone directly challenged a fellow member. Jack began: 'I don't accept the authority of the Bible.' At which Emily interrupted with 'at all?' Jack continued, 'and I wouldn't choose *Great Expectations*, but I would choose Dostoyevsky ... all I mean is I don't think of the Bible having that sort of authority over me – I'm a free man.' Emily's interruption didn't become an issue as she quickly moved to build bridges with Jack:

I think perhaps, if I'm picking you up correctly, you're not understanding authority in the way I meant it. I suppose, what I mean,
authority is a difficult word ... I mean it has [been], it is our
sacred text – it is one vehicle by which God makes himself known
to us. And therefore we take it seriously and we expect it to have a
resonance with the [?] of our lives in the way we wouldn't expect
Great Expectations or even Dostoyevsky – but there's something
qualitatively different [about] the Bible because of how it came
to be and the stories it tells and because of the message and the
revelation that it seeks to convey that's different to other ... so
that's what I meant by authority, not that it's coming ...

Fences were mended as Jack responded, 'I think I agree – I reacted
too hastily because I accept what you're saying.' Emily wanted to
ensure that she wasn't being mistaken for a certain type of Christian:

Authority is a difficult word and if I was a conservative Evangelical sitting here talking of the authority of scripture then I
would be saying then that we believe literally what it says – and
that's not what I mean. (Emily)

Later reflections

I invited the group to email any further reflections on the process that occurred to them after a gap of a few days. Not having a
participant who was openly and firmly in the Unionist camp was
noted, and generally the participants were grateful for the opportunity to explore the topic in this way. It was particularly important
to Harry that this approach allowed time for exchanging views
that did not have to be 'condensed into sound bites' and could be
'developed further as the process went on'. Jack felt able to say,
'I haven't enjoyed or been challenged so much by Bible study for
ages!' Charlie noted that not only could they introduce biblical
texts 'without it feeling contrived', but 'at one point were able to
articulate that it felt like this would be a contrived process – and we
were able to explore that too'. For Emily it was having the biblical

section in the middle rather than as a starting point, which 'meant the biblical passages were speaking into our context rather than defining the limits of the discussion'. Jessica felt she had gained 'confidence and some skills to open up and be part of discussions on the Referendum in everyday life'.

Discussion

We learn some things about Practical Theology and about the Referendum debate. What we have to take away regarding the discipline is first and foremost the suspicion, if not cynicism, that it has garnered from some who have encountered it in academic settings. It may be that lay people will not carry those same negative perceptions. To let them discover how beneficial Practical Theology can be could be an easier task than trying to preach to the (academic) choir. This group meeting on one Saturday, of mostly strangers, is a very hopeful sign that a quite non-directive, but still guided, conversation holds great potential for exploring a complex and tendentious topic. Of course, deploying Groome's method in other ways would likely include more formal input that would deepen the social analysis, biblical reflection and consequent critical dialogue. However, the lack of speaking *at* people appeared to give the space that members of this group so much appreciated. They were telling stories, not just sharing opinions. It ought not to escape our notice that some of this involved participants making themselves really quite vulnerable to others in the group. It seems to me that providing safe space enables people to explore the emotional dimensions of a topic; we just need to notice how many times fear could be mentioned, and sometimes a person's own, not merely their projections on to society at large.

The sequence confirmed what Groome and theological educators like him have known for years. Placing the biblical engagement after personal and social analysis frees the group to a considerable extent from the tramlines of constraining exegesis. Such an approach is not going to suit those for whom reader-response to the text is at best distracting and at worse heading off over the horizon of doctrinal error. My own experience in university teaching using Groome's method makes me all too aware that some Christians get very edgy if we don't immediately get to the Bible. They'll accept a short ice-breaker activity as a way of getting people talking, but holding back on discussing the Bible until we might have an inkling of the deeper issues at stake is really quite difficult. In this respect alone, Practical Theologians need to hold their nerve and not be coerced into an applied-theology method.

On the issue of Scottish Independence itself we learn quite a few things too. Fear is clearly significant; over not only what a 'Yes' might hold, but of the process of engaging in discussions that are so contentious. Uncertainty over the theological validity of a concept and attitudes falling under the broad banner of nationalism was also floating around. The very recent book by Doug Gay – not published until about two months after this study day – will be helpful for those wanting to think through a theology of nationalism.[7]

Values – particularly around social justice – were much more important to this group who made scarcely any mention of constitutional issues. The nearest they got to the constitution was what we might call subsidiarity; decisions taken as close as possible to the local arenas where the outcomes will be felt. If this group are in any way representative of wider opinion in Scotland, then it is, for many, a case of examining their vision of the sort of Scotland in which they wish to live. To a considerable extent this is Gay's approach, but also particularly so in the only other recent extended theological treatment of the debate – Donald Smith's *Freedom and Faith*.[8]

It was indeed the case that there was no one in the group beating the drum for the Union in quite the way that Jack was. However, the British case got a good airing, and it seemed obvious to me that all the participants were quite adept at handling their variants of Scottish, British or European identities. Ian Bradley, the author of a book published in 2007 on the spiritual identity of Britishness,

7 Doug Gay, *Honey from the Lion: Christianity and the Ethics of Nationalism*, London: SCM Press, 2013.

8 Donald Smith, *Freedom and Faith: A Question of Scottish Identity*, Edinburgh: Saint Andrew Press, 2013.

would find much among this group to support his perspective.[9] Suspicion over constitutional guarantees that can be muddied by politics also comes as no surprise in the current climate.

What is ostensibly a very simple five-step process has enabled this group to explore their views on Scottish Independence at a considerable depth. The very absence of expert opinion speaking *at* them turned out to be quite significant in allowing emotional and intellectual space – and not just time – for reflection. I am not at all suggesting that this format ought to replace sophisticated practical theological learning and research at undergraduate, postgraduate and postdoctoral levels. The point of this case study was a simple one – to demonstrate the potential of even a lightly guided conversation using a model of practical theological reflection. Now, having named my own experience of the discipline and having brought you a glimpse of how others have responded to the Practical Theology process, it is time to turn to the underpinning and the shape of the emphases that I believe require to be foregrounded for advancing the field. With Practical Theology giving so much attention to action, we need to be clearer about just what 'action' is before turning to 'critical discipleship' that, if I might be so bold, is Practical Theology in the Gospels.

---

9 Ian Bradley, *Believing in Britain: The Spiritual Identity of 'Britishness'*, London: I. B. Taurus, 2007.

4

Critical Discipleship

Action is relational

The scope of Practical Theology reaches well beyond the confines of pastoral care or other church-facing and church-directed activities. This is all well and good, but we need to dig more deeply, albeit making the matter more complicated, so that we can better understand what it is upon which we are exerting our capacity to reflect. To put it another way, how do we act? But this rather presupposes that we know what an 'act' is. As ever, it is far from obvious.

If we visit Westminster Abbey in London, the Place du Congrès in Brussels or the Arc de Triomphe in Paris (to mention only a few similar sites around the world), we can take a moment or two at the Tomb of the Unknown Soldier. Here are buried the remains of one or more servicemen (I'm not aware if any of these are women), who couldn't be identified through fatal injuries sustained in the First World War. From one perspective such tombs are memorials to all killed in that war, and later wars, who could not be named and buried. For grieving families in the immediate decades, such tombs also provided a focal point and perhaps a hint of the nation's gratitude. Viewed from another angle, Hannah Arendt argues that these tombs plead that the deaths of millions over those four years were *actions*.[1] It was, and likely continues to be, too awful to be left with nameless, mechanized, depersonalized outcomes from the making of war. In facing off against enemies there may be many words attached to sorties and bombardments in order to deceive the enemy or to bolster the morale of one's own troops. To describe

---

1 Hannah Arendt, *The Human Condition*, second edn, Chicago: University of Chicago Press, 1998 [1958], pp. 180–1.

circumstances in terms of 'died in action' is not only a means of differentiating – and honouring – a fatality during combat. 'Died in action' is also a claim that an action *with meaning* occurred. It was more than military activity, but a 'who' was disclosed in his or her unique particularity. Modern warfare strips action of this vital dimension and leaves behind the tragedy of achievements – which can be acknowledged and even honoured, but that do not restore the dignity of the one who has died.

This may seem a strange, even obtuse, illustration to bring into our discussion, but Arendt's perceptiveness pushes us to unpack quite what *action* might be. Action, for Arendt, is relational. She identifies three 'fundamental human activities', which correspond to the three basic conditions in which we experience life.[2] So, we have labour, work and action. *Labour* is our activity in our biological condition. This is our basic connection with nature through which we feed and sustain our bodies. When we talk about labouring, we customarily stop short of referring to what results from this; we keep the product as the outcome of *work*.[3] Labouring here is not intended in its metaphorical sense, such as when we talk about labouring up a hill when out for a run. Arendt wants to hold us, for a moment, in the realm of our individual activities that keep us, biological beings, alive.[4] We can, or be forced to, labour together (a chain-gang is perhaps the most extreme example), but instead of our being brought to deeper awareness of who we are as persons we lose our sense of identity as, to interpret Arendt, we are cogs on a gear wheel.[5]

In Arendt's scheme, *work* means making things. We construct or fabricate a world of buildings, transport and equipment of all kinds that take us far from the natural world.[6] Yet, work also speaks of a disposition. Everything is made into means towards our ends; we instrumentalize – and not only what we construct, but the very earth upon which we finally depend.[7] This is the charge

2 Arendt, *Human Condition*, p. 7.
3 Arendt, *Human Condition*, p. 80.
4 Arendt, *Human Condition*, p. 212.
5 Arendt, *Human Condition*, p. 213.
6 Arendt, *Human Condition*, p. 7.
7 Arendt, *Human Condition*, p. 156.

that environmentalists make against the destruction of fragile eco-systems for commercial advantage. Such treatment of the natural world is bad enough, but Arendt sees that our problem goes much deeper still. She is not against the notion of us using means to achieve particular ends, but Arendt argues that this disposition or attitude of instrumentalizing spills out of its appropriate container as we apply it in the wrong sphere: 'The issue at stake is ... the generalization of the fabrication experience in which usefulness and utility are established as the ultimate standards for life and the world.'[8] Fabrication (not with connotations of fibbing as we some-times use the term) leaks into and pollutes our world of *actions*.

Action is the realm of relationships between people who recog-nize one another as persons and who seek to enhance one another *as people*. We are familiar, perhaps, with the feeling that an employer is 'just using me' or a partner or one-time friend 'treats me like a stepping stone to what he wants'. For Arendt, it is speech *and* action (our making what we do understandable to one another) that enhances rather than degrades our personhood: 'Through [speech and action] [people] distinguish themselves instead of being merely distinct; they are the modes in which human beings appear to each other, not as physical objects, but *qua* [human].'[9] In activity we are disclosed as 'who' rather than as 'what'.[10] We ought not to think that Arendt is only referring to some interior attitude or sensation. There is a depth of embodied, mutual, active engagement. Such 'togetherness' is something we recognize, sadly perhaps because it can be all too fleeting, when we realize that we are 'with' people 'and neither for nor against them'.[11] Arendt, long before we talked commonly of worldwide webs of digital communication, termed this reality of being together as humans rather than as objects, as the '"web" of human relationships'.[12]

Action is *relational*, or as Robert Mager helpfully interprets

---

8 Arendt, *Human Condition*, p. 157.
9 Arendt, *Human Condition*, p. 176. Arendt uses the grammatically correct but now dated 'men' to refer to the whole of humanity.
10 Arendt, *Human Condition*, p. 179.
11 Arendt, *Human Condition*, p. 180.
12 Arendt, *Human Condition*, p. 183.

Arendt: 'Action is *interaction,* through which human beings both *reveal* and *realize* themselves publicly.'[13] Now, looking back to the Tomb of the Unknown Soldier, we catch a glimpse of that pressing need, especially for the recently bereaved in the 1920s and 1930s, to ground the loss of life in the web of human relationships. To contemplate that 'unknown' was truly so would have meant the deaths of millions were fabrications (work) rather than actions.

Deciding to act

If indeed action is relational and embedded in the web of human relationships, how do we decide how to act? We might adopt one of two main theories: that of economists who tell us that we make rational choices based upon our preferences and the available options, or that of many sociologists who see us following the norms of society. However, these are insufficient explanations, so let me describe a trip I occasionally make to one particular shop in Edinburgh.

Maplin, possibly more familiar in other cities as the similar Radioshack, is in the Haymarket area of the capital. Maplin is the place for we who like small electronic gadgets to get our 'fix'. Computer 'bits' sit alongside microphones, domestic CCTV systems, digital thermometers, soldering electronics projects and, strategically sited in the window, remote controlled cars and now helicopters with integral webcams. DJs can check out mixing decks and geeks can at least imagine how great our home security system will be when we rig our lights and heating to our iPhone and control our personal drone surveillance system. Among us boys searching for new toys, there can be one or two women shopping in Maplin, because, after all, we're not quite so nerdy as the young men in the comic book store![14] Sometimes I need a visit to Maplin.

---

13 Robert Mager, 'Do We Learn to Know God from What We Do? A Plea for a Relational Concept of Action', in Elaine Graham and Anna Rowlands (eds), *Pathways to the Public Square*, Münster: Lit Verlag, 2005, p. 196.

14 I know I'm exaggerating the gendered consumer experience, but this is still a pretty accurate representation.

I'm not crossing town because I already know what I need – or even if I need anything. Nor is it because I *want* a particular gadget. *It's only once there that I'll know if I need something.*

What I've described is the theory of action that Hans Joas has propounded as not just another alongside economists' rational-actor and sociologists' normative choice. Rather, Joas offers what he considers to be a theory that overarches the other two, because his claim is that 'there is a creative dimension to all human action'.[15] Joas argues that rational-choice and normative models of action are fixated on a concept of rationality that conceals important, flawed assumptions. First, they assume that I am able to be intentional in the sense that I set goals that I wish to achieve and select the means to attain them. Second, that I am able to control my body, making it an instrument of my means and ends. Third, that I can act autonomously towards other people and my environment.[16] At first sight, these three assumptions seem common sense, but they begin to unravel on closer inspection.

As John Dewey argued in the 1920s, goals are not simply antici-pations of what I bring into being in the future. Rather, 'goals belong to the present'.[17] Goals *emerge* as I consider what means are available to me in specific situations. As Joas puts it, '[g]oal-setting does not take place as a cognitive act prior to action but is based on prereflective aspirations that are operative in the action situation'.[18] Lying further behind the assumption that Joas is chal-lenging is the notion that acting is a series of unitary (stop-start as it were) acts: 'I was sitting in my chair, now I act.'[19] Instead, claims Joas, 'we are acting in a course of action'.[20] Were we to pause in

15 Hans Joas and Jens Beckert, 'Action Theory', in J. H. Turner (ed.), *Handbook of Sociological Theory*, New York: Kluwer Academic / Plenum Publishers, 2001, p. 270.

16 Joas and Beckert, 'Action Theory', p. 272.

17 See Joas and Beckert, 'Action Theory', p. 273. Their reference is to John Dewey, *Experience and Nature*, London: Open Court, 1958 [1925].

18 Joas and Beckert, 'Action Theory', p. 273.

19 Hans Joas, 'Action Is the Way in Which Humans Beings Exist in the World – Interview', Dialog On Leadership http://www.iwp.jku.at/born/mpwfst/o2/www.dialogonleadership.org/Joasx1999.html#nine.

20 Joas, 'Action Is the Way'.

our chairs to be aware of our thoughts we would likely find that we are working through multiple (perhaps innumerable) perceptions of our surroundings that have an impact upon what we next (or rather continue to) do. Joas refers to door handles that we are able to recognize as having a function and not ornamentation – otherwise we'd have no way of getting out through the door. We could add to that observations about the traction offered by the rug at our feet, the panting of our dog hoping for a walk, and the light inside and outside the room. We could go on and on. Joas's point is well made – we should really talk of action rather than acts.[21]

Our control over our body is not quite what rational-actor and normative-choice models assume either. Finding sleep is not going to be achieved by repeating to ourselves, 'I want to fall asleep.' Laughing and weeping, in other respects, slip through any claims to being able to control our bodies.[22] These features of our corporeality points Joas to an aspect that is actually much more important for his argument. He wants to explain how our bodies are to be integrated into a theory of action. His route is body-image: how we subjectively experience our own body.

I recall a television documentary that took us behind the scenes of a clothing shop to find that fitting room mirrors were mounted with a downwards tilt to offer a more flattering reflection to the shopper – and in carefully managed lighting conditions. Our body-image is constructed through our interactions with other people. Taunts at adolescent growth spurts or 'puppy fat' come to be replaced by distanced but equally powerful messages that, to a greater or lesser extent, we absorb or repudiate. Here, with Joas, we approach the third flawed assumption: our autonomy. Being who we are – including the choices we make – is a profoundly social experience. Furthermore, we are never finished with making ourselves through our interactions with others doing likewise.

Joas's claim is that action is best understood as creativity. This is not to dismiss the fact that we act with different levels of creativity at various times. Some people, it seems, are more creative than

---

21 See also Hans Joas, *The Creativity of Action*, trans. Jeremy Gaines and Paul Keast, Cambridge: Polity Press, 1996, p. 157.

22 Joas and Beckert, 'Action Theory', p. 275.

others.[23] What is of most interest to me is the fundamental place that Joas gives to *reflection*:

> Reflection is the intermediate phase in the process of action. We are constantly in the processes of action when we've encountered a problem for attention; reflection is action. It's interrupted, we have no choice but to reflect, otherwise we would constantly reproduce the same problem. So it is a phase in action, it's an immediate phase in action. In this phase we discover, sometimes in surprising ways, our pre-reflective impulses, conceptions, and so on.[24]

Joas pulls action into the realm of perception of our surroundings, but with a very strong emphasis on embodiment and social relations. Similarly, Arendt's notion of action within a web of human relationships grounds our valuing of sociality as integral to not merely knowing what to do, but who I am as the one-with-others who is acting.[25] What does a theory of action as creativity (Joas) and within a web of human relationships (Arendt) mean for Christian discipleship? Looking from this direction will let us see how Practical Theology is vital not merely as an analysis of practice, but as a dimension of what it means to be Christian.

Reflection in the Gospels

We all know people who might warrant the designation 'critical disciple'. They're anything but the cheeriest of souls as nothing is ever quite right from their perspective. The sermon is too long – or too short. The music is too traditional – or not traditional enough. The church building is too cold, the pews are too uncomfortable, or 'the same people get asked to help all the time'. God forbid that

23 Joas and Beckert, 'Action Theory', p. 284.

24 Joas, 'Action Is the Way'.

25 For a development of a relational model of action in the context of Practical Theology, see Robert Mager, 'Action Theories', in Bonnie J. Miller-McLemore (ed.), *The Wiley-Blackwell Companion to Practical Theology*, Chichester: Wiley-Blackwell, 2012, pp. 255–65.

we might, on an off-day, be counted among them. Gathered at the celestial river the critical disciple will probably find the eschatological waters a tad on the chilly side. There's a famous cartoon that appeared in *Leadership*, the US evangelical journal, back in the 1980s. By Erik and Vicki Johnson, this cartoon showed a senior pastor with heavy jowls turning to his fresh-faced young colleague and saying, 'Ever had one of those days when you felt you just had to rebuke someone?'[26] He is evidently the patron saint of all those critical disciples who can only ever find fault. This is not the sense in which I am thinking of 'critical discipleship'.

Neither do I have in mind the jeremiad for whom the whole world is heading to hell in a handcart; the cart being accelerated with every announcement of a progressive social policy that constrains conservative Christians from imposing their moral agenda on people at large. Again, we know the type for whom equal marriage for gay or lesbian people, women's rights, multiculturalism or Sunday shopping make up a litany of evils that depart from 'Christian standards'. Perhaps they could be designated 'complaining disciples', and, yes, more progressive and liberal Christians are not immune from these habits either.

The picture I have been building of Practical Theology is a theory of action that points towards a rather different sense of the term 'critical discipleship'. It is a form of Christian discipleship that takes reflection on practice, context and faith seriously. Critical discipleship appreciates that our goals and our means emerge from our perception of our situations. Critical discipleship treats the web of human relationships in which we perform actions as a fabric that can be stained or ripped by dispositions appropriate to the arenas of work and labour. Discerning what is leaching through the porous boundaries of our complex lives together is a vital dimension of recognizing where and how others (and we ourselves) are being degraded, constrained and diminished in our potential to flourish in God's world.

---

26 Erik and Vicki Johnson, 'Pastor's Bad Day', *Leadership Journal*, http://www.christianitytoday.com/le/2004/may-online-only/pastors-bad-day.html.

The cantankerous disciple finding fault in church and the denouncing disciple contending with the world do, however, have a point. Both Church and world are situations in which we act (in the sense that Arendt and Joas have helped us identify). Similarly, these situations shape us: our goals, expectations, self-image and identity. Non-theological models of action demand that we develop our reflective, critical capacities. Are there pointers from within the gospel itself that raise similar expectations? In other words, is the 'critical' of 'critical discipleship' an adjective added only because a political philosopher and a social theorist endorse it as a capacity that people in general need to develop?

'Discipleship' is one of those words that is, to twist the hymn, weak and heavy laden, cumbered with a load of care. The term strains under insinuations (and perhaps too often fairly so) of indoctrination, or at least a highly didactic induction into what a particular Christian community considers to be a 'good Christian life'. Attempts to sustain commitment – disciples not just converts – can be highly detailed and enthusiastic, but somewhat programmatic. For just how many 'new' discipleship courses can there possibly be a need? Granted, media mutate at an alarming rate and all but a very few Christian courses and accompanying materials do look out of date very quickly. (Whether they were ever at the cutting-edge of artistic design and educational theory is another matter altogether.)

I think it fair to say that most discipleship programmes tilt towards teaching the liturgical patterns of a community to newcomers along with expectations of 'good' Christian behaviour and some grasp of doctrinal 'hot-button' issues. I do acknowledge the difference between a course for enquirers (who are given the opportunity to ask questions and consider a faith commitment) and a programme for those who have, in one way or another, aligned themselves with Christ and his Church. I am, for these purposes, not considering enquirers, although I am well aware that the boundary between enquirer and disciple is one that is not to be drawn in ink but in pencil.

It is easy to see how 'discipleship' is heavy laden, when traditional images loom so vividly. Jesus' Twelve left their trades and followed him – into costly conflict. The New Testament Epistles are, to state the obvious, letters to Christian communities finding themselves quite often torn between rival leaders and mutually contradictory teachings. Unrepentant sinners are to be expelled lest they lead others astray. False teachers and their credentials are marginalized if not wholly repudiated.

To characterize the New Testament Church in terms of what we would recognize as a franchise would be grossly inaccurate, but I will go ahead anyway. Fred's Pizzas is the brand and corporate infrastructure with the benefits of national or global marketing. Buying a franchise to run a Fred's Pizza in the Newington area of Edinburgh requires baking pizzas to the brand's dimensions, quality and appearance. So too with the signage, staff uniforms and outfitting of the premises. The New Testament Church was clearly not homogenized to this extent, for it showed considerable regional and cultural variations. Yet discipleship was about incorporation into a community of congregations that understood itself as sharing much doctrine (in as much as it was yet defined), ethos, practices and, significantly, delegated authority from valid apostles. Perhaps the model we can best lay over a network of 2,000 years ago is that of degree-awarding universities; independent entities in many respects, but mutually accountable through systems of peer review. The University of Exeter is free to develop its own specialities and regional emphases, but is recognizably similar to the University of Edinburgh. (Tempting as it is to draw tenuous parallels between political interference in universities of the twenty-first century and the early Church of the second and subsequent centuries, this would take us rather off the point.)

The New Testament Church is not like the ideal that Evangelicals, Catholics, Liberals, Pentecostals or Emergentists each would prefer it had been.[27] Yet, the practice of induction or catechesis clearly involved hierarchical (arguably patriarchal) communication of authorized teachings and the formation of people into validated social mores. It is a world uninformed by our educational philosophies that favour exploration, student-centred

---

27 By 'Emergentists' I simply mean those who have aligned themselves with the 'Emergent Church' concept.

learning and rigorous critical questioning. To put it bluntly, I doubt that the apostle Paul would have had much time for the more radical methods of practical-theological reflection and education that I am advancing in this book.[28] Preaching at such length that it cost Eutychus his life (albeit temporarily) is not a learning style easily squared with our ideologies.[29] Nor would Paul's repudiation of those who disagree with him comfortably fit Freire's (nor probably Groome's) models.[30]

However, as dissimilar as the models of learning and teaching might be, I suggest that Jesus had set up a way of being a disciple that had to incorporate what we would now call 'reflection'.[31] As much as I would like to claim Jesus as the first Christian Practical Theologian, I shall not go quite that far. To find traces of an impetus towards critical reflection in Jesus' call to discipleship is not to read his life and ministry through this one, anachronistic lens. But if everyone always reads Jesus through one or more lenses we might as well add Practical Theology to the mix. Jesus' critical take on forms of Jewish religion in his time are easy to demonstrate as demanding what we now call reflection. So, taking the more difficult first, we can consider hints from Jesus that think of world-facing critical reflection.

The not-quite-rich young men

Jesus' hyperbole in responding to the rich young ruler's question about how he might be saved gives Christians plenty of scope for avoiding vows of poverty as normative. Giving his wealth away to the poor so that he might enter the kingdom of God faced this par-

28 However, for a different view, although it is not exactly around the same model of Practical Theology as here, see Nigel Rooms, 'Paul as Practical Theologian: *Phronesis* in Philippians', *Practical Theology* 5.1 (2012), pp. 81–94.

29 See Acts 20.8–10.

30 Nevertheless, Groome is a Roman Catholic educator, who is keenly aware of the authority of Tradition and Scripture; his is not a cavalier approach that leaves everything to readers' interpretations.

31 My aim here is not to simply link contemporary Practical Theology with the ancient and lasting tradition of *phronesis* or practical wisdom.

ticular young man with his attachment to riches – if we take the common line that leaves the advantage with those who use their riches compassionately. But if we assume that other rich young men witnessed, or were later told about this encounter, what might be required of them? Let's say they were not quite so rich as the man in the Gospel story. It was clear that some of Jesus' followers did not dispose of the entirety of their wealth (since his ministry was supported by various women).[32] After the crucifixion we find that some of the disciples return to their fishing businesses so we can reasonably infer that they themselves had not disposed of *all* their assets. So young men not quite so rich as the man who questioned Jesus about salvation would have to ask themselves a few questions. What assets do I have, and what is the cut-off value that would define *me* as rich? As 'rich' is a relative evaluation – if not even quite subjective – do I qualify as one who has to divest himself of his riches in order to enter the kingdom of God? Young men towards the lower end of the scale that might be classed as 'rich' can ask themselves these questions, but answers are more difficult to articulate.

Of course, someone with only a very limited purse could be deeply attached to his money. The widow putting her mite in the offering is the counterexample.[33] My point is simply that Jesus' response to one rich young man demands quite sophisticated reflection on personal finances and the social context in which they are valued on the part of other men unsure about quite where they fall on the prosperity index. Their assessment of their own wealth could not be an entirely interior, and in that sense spiritualized, process. Their like are confronted with a potentially complex consideration of the economic context of their own communities.

The lounge lizard pensioner

Squabbles over family inheritance claims usually advantage no one but the lawyers paid to help in the adjudication process. For other reasons Jesus resists being drawn into one such dispute and

---

32 See Luke 8.3.
33 Mark 12.41–4; Luke 21.1–4.

instead tells a parable – one that I can imagine did not go down well with the prospective appellant. Jesus homes in on the greed that he discerns lies behind the man's demand for part of the family inheritance. The parable is the one we tend to know as 'the rich fool'.[34] Careful tending of his land – and perhaps not a little good fortune – results in a man securing an abundant crop beyond what he can sell in one season. His plan is to build a bigger barn and, at least for a period, retire; his pension safely stored. God calls the man a fool – I'm not sure it's because the pensioner has made provision for his future. Rather, it's what he does in retirement – 'eat, drink and be merry' – that brings God's censure in the parable. His folly is sitting back, and he is a paradigm for those who, as Jesus interprets his own parable, 'store up treasures for themselves but are not rich towards God'.[35]

Like the not-quite-so-rich young men, people and especially the would-be appellant are confronted with family dynamics, lifestyle choices, investing in the future *as well as* matters usually designated more directly spiritual.

The occasion and the parable itself anticipate reflection on the part of hearers who will face inheritance questions within their own families – sooner or later. The point at which investment slips over into greed is contextual and subjective. Few might have the opportunity to be tempted to live off a pension and be whatever the first-century equivalent of a lounge lizard might look like. However, reflection upon their and their dependants' future is incumbent upon them – for not everyone dies the day they sign a pension plan. The context of their reflection is the vagaries of an agricultural economy – complicated surely by enemy occupation by the Romans and their vassals.

The blessed

Jesus' Beatitudes (Matt. 5.3–12) are so familiarly deployed as consolation in loss and exhortation to traditional piety that these

---

34 Luke 12.13–21.
35 Luke 12.21 NRSV.

sayings are not readily associated with the reflective, critical stance of Practical Theology. Admittedly, our friends living under economic and political oppression have drawn from this deep well in developing a spirituality of Liberation Theology, but arguably this is much less the case in privileged contexts.[36] My point is simply that the Beatitudes rather presuppose the capacity to engage in what we call critical reflection.

Being 'poor in spirit' is not a quantifiable term; there were, and are, no indices of 'poverty in spirit'. Taking this to describe the experience of being crushed by oppression to the point that hope is all but extinguished, it is not self-evident to whom this might refer. Careful consideration of the 'web of human relationships' (to reiterate Arendt) is necessary to make pastoral–political sense of the blessing that is the promised kingdom of God.

Similarly, mourning and meekness are, in each their own way, complex actions and attitudes. Just as showing mercy and making peace, let alone thirsting for righteousness, demand being attuned to immediate situations, the Beatitudes thrust hearers into a mode of reflection. I think this is more than simply acknowledging the ethical complexity and nuanced responses that the Beatitudes encapsulate. These sharply concise sayings are but the starting point or impetus for deeper exploration of one's own and others' actions (again in the sense that Arendt defines action). Immediately we are confronted with questions such as who, then, is meek? What is peace-making?

Formation in the Gospels

These few examples, that we more traditionally have come to know as the 'rich young ruler' and the 'rich fool', work – rhetorically if you will – rather like the Beatitudes. Each call forth world-facing critical reflection – a stance that although interpreted with great diversity within the Christian community, is generally not controversial. Christians get the point that we are to be critical

---

36 Gustavo Gutiérrez, *We Drink from Our Own Wells*, London: SCM Press, 2005.

of where 'the world' is mistaken, malevolent or neglectful. That a critical stance is required *towards our own faith* is not a notion that is always quite so obvious or encouraged. I am not thinking here of the predilection to criticize *others'* Christian tradition – that common strategy for differentiating ourselves and justifying our own denominational preferences. What I have in mind is discipleship that is inherently critical of one's *own* faith. To put it more radically than this, my relationship with Christ needs to be one that maintains some measure of critical distance. I am going to adopt a two-pronged defence of this admittedly contentious assertion. Sociologist and philosopher Michel Foucault will help me demonstrate the importance of appreciating how we are being shaped but there are hints within the Gospels endorsing the qualification of language of 'total surrender' that makes many Christians so uncomfortable about being critical of Jesus himself.

Foucault and formation

Foucault is perhaps best known in theological circles for his trenchant critique of disciplinary mechanisms such as religion, education, the prison and professional guilds.[37] The Catholic confessional, the Puritan pastor's house-calls, and the evangelical Bible study and prayer meeting may have the worthiest of intentions for the godly formation of intelligent people, but it is not difficult to take cheap, easy shots at Christian practices that too readily give scope for abusive, domineering behaviour. Instead, I want to draw on Foucault's identification of what he calls 'the care of the self' – practices and a disposition that he has traced from antiquity.

In asking 'who am I?' the structures, systems, symbols and traditions that have formed me as an ethical subject need to be disclosed to me. If I am going to consciously practise freedom, then it is part of the ethical task to take care of myself. Only thereby might I care for others. Who I am is really a number of relationships that I have

---

37 Michel Foucault, *Discipline and Punish: The Birth of the Prison*, London: Penguin Books, 1977.

with myself in any number of given situations.[38] For example, the form I take as a political subject when voting is quite different to the form I take when seeking sexual fulfilment. How these various forms of the subject are constituted in relation to what Foucault calls 'games of truth' is part of ethical inquiry – of caring for myself.[39] In other words, I take responsibility for interrogating the relations of power in which I am being shaped.[40] Foucault wants us to know about our situation – and particularly how we are being exploited. To act ethically therefore involves acquiring knowledge of and facility with the rules of managing one another and the *ethos* (the practice of the self) 'that', he says, 'will allow us to play these games of power with as little domination as possible'.[41]

How, then, does this connect with the notion of being formed as Christians; as disciples of Christ? Our shaping – what for our purposes we can talk of as formation – occurs within relations of power. Most obviously these include our pastor, preacher, priest and other influential Christians around us. However, we ought not to forget other relations of power such as family, friends, local and national politicians, the police and entertainment moguls. While all these are actual people, their influence and our relations of power are, to greater or lesser extents, mediated through the social, political, economic and cultural structures that surround us. Foucault would have the person in formation discover or realize how it is that she is being shaped by relations of power – not merely power deployed over her, but her own relations of power deployed towards other people.

This may not be as straightforward as it appears. Foucault is alert to the dynamic within relations of power as always those of acquiescence *and* resistance. Our response is, however, constrained not only by structural aspects such as denominational doctrinal

---

38 Michel Foucault, 'The Ethics of the Concern for Self as a Practice of Freedom', in R. Rabinow (ed.), *Michel Foucault. Ethics: Subjectivity and Truth: The Essential Works of Foucault 1954–1984, Vol. 1*, London: Penguin Books, 2000, p. 290.
39 Foucault, 'Ethics', p. 282.
40 Foucault, 'Ethics', p. 292.
41 Foucault, 'Ethics', p. 298.

statements and conditions of membership. It is our internalizing of the disciplinary mechanisms that is Foucault's other significant disclosure. We take on board the messages of obedience, conformity and acquiescence, and our self-image assumes these characteristics – *to the extent that we do not notice them.* In other words, the structures of discipline cease to be predominantly material institutions or persons, and instead we internalize their control over us. While for some people this is to see themselves as an underclass with no political agency, others conceive of themselves as patients who have no choice but to submit to the medical profession.

Christian people internalize the disciplinary mechanisms of their congregation (whether or not the denominational system is hierarchal, associational, loose or rigid) to the extent that they may be oblivious to how they are being shaped. Unless we adopt a critical perspective there can be little chance of adequately disclosing the internalizing of the disciplinary mechanisms in which we live our week-by-week Christian lives.[42] If it were just that critical distance is needed from the *structures* of practising the faith, my point might be challenging enough. I think, however, we need to go further and think in this light about our relationships with God.

First, let me offer a bit of theological context. *Agape* is a treasured pillar of how Christians have understood God's unconditional love and that quality of love that we ought to mirror towards one another. Certain notions of agapic love have been problematic when regard for another person (other-regard) is set as paradigmatic. Foreshadowing later feminist criticisms, Martin D'Arcy, at the end of the 1940s, argued for self-regard to be a legitimate aspect of agape. While the tendency has been for *agape* to be treated by way of the doctrine of atonement, D'Arcy instead framed it within the mutuality of the Trinity.[43] Barbara Andolsen recognizes the important difference here. The full surrender of Christ's self to crucifixion, if it is allowed to exclusively set the parameters of agape, very

---

42 I am not dispensing with the idea of legitimate authority and merely putting it under the heading of power; assuming power to be always bad.

43 Martin C. D'Arcy, *The Mind and Heart of Love*, London: Faber & Faber, 1946. Quoted in Barbara Hilkert Andolsen, 'Agape in Feminist Ethics', *Journal of Religious Ethics* 9.1 (1981), pp. 72–3.

readily suggests self-abnegation for anyone who 'lays down his life' to follow him. The particular problem for women had been recognized by some female theologians long before the feminist movement of the 1960s.[44] Andolsen presents a sermon by Anna Howard Shaw, preached in 1893, where Shaw alerts women to be wary of demands that they sacrifice their own self-development for the sake of a male relative.[45] This echoes down the decades and we today are hopefully much more attuned to the gendering of Christian discipleship.

However, even if Feminist Theologians have partly succeeded in breaking the link between godliness for women and giving of themselves for others without reserve, the problematic framework lives on. It is still obvious in conservative Christian models of the 'Christian wife' and 'Christian mother'. My contention is that the language of surrender and obedience – framed by the faithfulness of Christ's embrace of his cross – inculcates reluctance to value the critical dimension of discipleship for everyone.

A shift from self-effacement towards 'the worth and sacredness of the self' is a process in Dietrich Bonhoeffer's journey that Lisa Dahill has helpfully articulated. From aspiring to being nothing but like the Beloved Disciple, Bonhoeffer (as he moves into the conspiracy to assassinate Hitler) makes more prominent his belief that discernment or self-examination 'is at the centre of the mature Christian life'.[46]

Postcolonial theologians make a related point when they regale against the imposition, through the canon of Western literature, of colonialist models of the exotic Other – be she Arab or be he African.[47] The master–servant (if not actually master–slave)

---

44 Mary Grey's essay on education is paradigmatic of this critique. Grey argues for redemption in education demanding self-affirmation, self-knowledge and mutual empowerment (Mary C. Grey, 'Feminist Images of Redemption in Education', *British Journal of Religious Education* 12.1 (1989), pp. 20–8).

45 Anna Howard Shaw, n. d., The Dillon Collection, the Shaw Series. Quoted in Andolsen, 'Agape', p. 75.

46 Lisa E. Dahill, *Reading from the Underside of Selfhood: Bonhoeffer and Spiritual Formation*, Eugene, OR: Pickwick Publications, 2009, p. 88.

47 See, for example, R. S. Sugirtharajah, *Postcolonial Reconfigurations:*

relationship of the civilizing colonial official or missionary towards indigenous communities inculcated and often internalized notions of Christian discipleship of unquestioning obedience to 'those who know best'.[48]

To gender and postcolonialist critiques we might add those of queer theologians. While the immediate challenge of queer theology is to heterosexual superiority, it is more fundamentally a challenge to any enforcing of normativity. Here, the statistical reality of a majority (even substantial majority) elides into an ideology where 'being normal' takes to itself the power to name what is deviant – with the moral and social opprobrium that follows.[49]

Feminist, postcolonial and queer theologies challenge – perhaps even subvert – traditional notions of the Christian disciple. It is, into conformity with Christ, that formation is directed and to which the predominant way of seeing requires modification. To put it another way, we bring preconceptions about discipleship into our understanding of what it means to be a faithful Christian. Feminist, postcolonial and queer theologies proffer us different lenses. Therefore, *now*, and only now, we turn to some biblical texts that suggest that *critical discipleship* need not rest on Foucault for its legitimation. We can start with a biblical narrative that seems more amenable to my proposal – the case of the 'uppity woman', also known as the Syrophoenician woman.

An Alternative Way of Reading the Bible and Doing Theology, London: SCM Press, 2003; Kwok Pui-Lan, 'Making the Connections: Postcolonial Studies and Feminist Biblical Interpretation', in R. S. Sugirtharajah (ed.), *The Postcolonial Biblical Reader*, Oxford: Blackwell, 2006.

48 Those of us familiar with 'missionary services' in the evangelical tradition will likely recall the accounts of self-sacrifice by young women called by God to the mission field. Yes, some told tales of wrestling with God about their vocation, but their preaching in their sending churches reinforced the discourse of submission; replicating the missionary society's long-held framing of discipleship for indigenous converts.

49 See, for example, Elizabeth Stuart, *Gay and Lesbian Theologies: Repetitions with Critical Difference*, Aldershot: Ashgate, 2003; Ken Stone, 'Border Anxiety: Food, Sex and the Boundaries of Identity', *Practising Safer Texts: Food, Sex and Bible in Queer Perspective*, London: T. & T. Clark, 2005, pp. 46–67.

The 'uppity woman'

A Gentile, Syrophoenician and thereby pagan woman approaches Jesus from a social position of considerable disadvantage (Mark 7.24–30; in Matt. 15.21–8 she is a Canaanite). The woman (in Matt. 15) is appealing to him on behalf of her sick daughter and met by silence from Jesus. 'I was sent only to the lost sheep of Israel' (Matt. 15.24) is Jesus' response to his disciples concurring with their plan to be rid of a woman who keeps shouting at him. She is, as Sharon Ringe has memorably named her, the 'uppity woman'.[50]

The Matthean text has her standing up to Jesus, refusing to accept his rebuttal as the final word. Her retort that even the dogs eat the crumbs from the master's table seems a brave public challenge to a young rabbi, who sees himself as ethnically superior.[51] Jesus' self-consciousness of his own mission is brought to book, found wanting, and altered by this encounter. Granted, this woman does not neatly fit the traditional concept of a disciple, so let me bring us closer to Jesus' immediate circle. First to his family and then to his innermost followers.

Jesus' family

In Mark 3 we find Jesus' family worried about the state of his mind – given that he has come home and crowds are gathering around him such that no one seems able to eat. No matter how important one's mission is, this chaos cannot continue indefinitely. Jesus' mother, brothers, and perhaps his sisters, come looking for him at one particular house. They stand outside and try to get a message in to him that they are here – presumably to get him to come and

---

50 Sharon H. Ringe, 'A Gentile Woman's Story', in Letty M. Russell (ed.), *Feminist Interpretation of the Bible*, Oxford: Blackwell, 1985, p. 65.

51 While some (indeed most) prefer to think of Jesus here as engaged in a friendly provocation that justifies a mission to the Gentile world, others find his mind being changed; see the discussion in Musa W. Dube, *Post-colonial Feminist Interpretation of the Bible*, St Louis, MI: Chalice Press, 2000, pp. 157–95.

eat with them. Jesus uses their concern as a teaching point to the crowd – assuring these followers of their special relationship with him; they are his family. This does not necessitate Jesus repudiating familial ties.

I think we can find hints here of a family reaching out to him – in other words, taking a critical, thoughtful, concerned stance towards what their brother is doing. To be honest, it has shades of what support groups might call 'an intervention'. He cannot go on this way; his current strategy is simply unsustainable. Now I don't want to read too much into the artificial chapter divisions in the compilation of the narrative. However, Mark 4 does open with 'Again he began to teach beside the sea'. Has Jesus responded to his family's concerns and even slightly modified his behaviour?

I acknowledge that there is a vast weight of tradition that seems to steer us away from thinking that Jesus would either have countenanced or needed critique from his disciples. The very idea of standing up to Jesus is bracketed with apostasy, disobedience, rebellion and lack of faith. But, I would suggest, that is the discourse of the powerful – of those who are in a position to define the 'normal Christian life'. And, we should remember, that the powerful can be very big fish in small ecclesial ponds!

My point is that we require critical distance from the formation in which we are being shaped. It is this subverting that enables us to see how we are being shaped. To qualify language of 'surrender' to Jesus, of being formed in his likeness, goes against the grain of the dominant modes of at least popular, if not well-tuned, Christian spirituality. Part of the reluctance I think lies in a cosmology within which evil is hypostatized – if not turned wholly into a person, Satan. With apocalyptic imagery coupled to pre-modern vulnerability, the Christian is set to choose between 'God and the devil'. To be a critical disciple in this vein is to be siding with the devil against God to whom obedience is due without reserve. Here we then come to the most problematic biblical episode for my case: Peter's confrontation with Jesus.

Jesus and Peter

Peter, you will remember, remonstrates with Jesus who has inti-
mated that suffering lies ahead in Jesus' journey to Jerusalem. Peter
contends that this cannot be allowed to happen, but Jesus turns on
him with the now famous injunction, 'Get behind me, Satan.'

> And Peter took him aside and began to rebuke him, saying,
> 'God forbid it, Lord! This must never happen to you.' But he
> turned and said to Peter, 'Get behind me, Satan! You are a
> stumbling-block to me; for you are setting your mind not on
> divine things but on human things.' (Matt. 16.22–23)

So much, you might say, for the notion of critical discipleship. Yet,
not all is quite what it *has* to seem like. If we can dial down our
conditioning to read this in semi-literal terms (by which I mean
hearing the echoes of pre-modern cosmological language), Peter
might not be seen here in quite such a bad light. The word 'Satan'
can simply refer to a stumbling block; it need not be invariably
hypostasized-evil.[52] Jesus uses language and imagery of his time.
Vividly, that is true; Jesus identifies Peter's remonstration as an
obstruction to what lies ahead – but I don't think we have to think that
Peter has been momentarily taken over by the devil as a mouthpiece.

Certainly, the obstruction is one that Jesus repudiates, but I
think we can cast Peter's intentions in a different light. Akin to
Jesus' family plans for an 'intervention', Peter is the caring friend
who sees his rabbi setting himself on a path of self-destruction.
What else would love demand of Peter other than he confront
Jesus and attempt to intervene? Peter has learned, from Jesus, the
importance of challenging acts of faith precisely because religion is
such a powerful force. Without Peter voicing his confrontation or
obstruction, how else would Jesus truly know that Peter loved him?
Peter loved Jesus enough to stand up to him; and we might say that
Jesus loved Peter too much to accede to that obstruction.

---

52 P. G. Maxwell-Stuart, *Satan: A Biography*, Stroud: Amberley Publishing, 2008, p. 19. For an extensive discussion, largely from a liberationist
perspective, see Miguel A. De La Torre and Albert Hernández, *The Quest
for the Historical Satan*, Minneapolis, MN: Fortress Press, 2011.

My point is that of all people, Jesus and Peter would have understood that uncritical submission to a religious vocation is foolhardy. If Christian discipleship is framed too tightly within language of obedience, submission and surrender, it is in danger of losing its criticality. This has been the imposed – and often internalized – experience of women, colonial subjects, queer, physically or cognitively disabled people, poor or racially stigmatized persons. Critical discipleship is not simply a humanist safeguard against the power of religion, it is, I suggest, integral to the gospel, because Jesus' ministry was not possible without the faithful, loving confrontation from those who cared most about him. They maintained critical distance from him – while loving him – by not accepting a frame of total surrender or unconditional obedience.

Summary

We have seen how action is a thoroughly relational concept and how integral is reflection to our embodied experience of the possibilities and constraints in which we live with others. We are creatively making ourselves through our interactions with other people who are doing likewise. Carrying this disposition of being critical into the frame of Christian discipleship I have suggested that it is implied in the Gospels. Jesus' use of parables demanded critical reflection on the part of his hearers, and this often seemed to be the questioning of economic and social categories and contexts. One way in which we can both learn and practise critical discipleship is by using a practical theological method – particularly one like that of Groome. What I am arguing in this book is that the discipline of Practical Theology requires to be made more accessible to people in order that they can *do* theology in their contexts. It is now time to turn to consider what might be some of the barriers inhibiting this wider disseminating of Practical Theology. First, we look at the challenge of professionalization, and in later chapters at how the field might be given a more radical edge to make our criticism of our contexts more liberative.

5

Professing to be Professional

I can claim, until I'm blue in the face, that I'm an expert on ninth-century Scottish poetry, but such assertions mean nothing without the validation of my peers. If I'm really smart, I focus on the work of a poet who only a very few people have heard of, so that my peers could meet in one of the few remaining telephone boxes that used to be a familiar sight on British streets. We three, deciding when we will meet again, could award ourselves the mutual recognition of being experts in this narrow field. But precious good it would do us because 'expert' is a relational category, not an objective one. Even were I to actually know anything about one ninth-century Scottish poet, a claim to be an expert would be to grossly mis-apply the common usage. It is the wider profession of historians – particularly specialists in Scottish literary history – who could give any meaning to expertise. Professions are the principal way in which society institutionalizes expertise; individuals and, it can be argued, very small coteries are not entitled to grant expert status on themselves or members of their tiny inner circle.

Even my fictitious example is not without its problems. Can expertise be claimed when the field of knowledge or skill is so very narrow that one's peers can be numbered on the fingers of one hand? In this case, expertise does indeed rely on relationships across fields of knowledge themselves, and not just the expert as a person. As a relative term, expertise is not dichotomous. Experts and lay persons sit on a gradient of knowledge and skill. To complicate matters still further there are other gradients in play: prestige, privileges and power.[1] From a sociological perspective, professions are 'forms of exclusion, separating experts from nonexperts'.[2]

The language of profession is ambivalent to Christian ears. Profession of holy orders – being set apart to an uncommon life – carries a long heritage. Treating priesthood and ordained ministry as professional bears connotations that conflict with vocation and hint at a cold detachment not considered fitting for this office. 'Expert' is substantially more problematic in most Christian circles. Modest self-effacement is preferred, but commitment and perceptivity are none the less valued and publicly affirmed. It could well be a cultural legacy that makes many British Christians look askance at the proliferation of 'experts' from the USA in mission, worship-leading or church leadership, who write books and give conference addresses. Strangely, or perhaps not, 'experts' in compassionate service to marginalized people or in contemplative lives of prayer are rather fewer on the ground. Their ministries, experience and sacrificial commitment might be honoured, but we recoil at tarnishing them with the accolade of 'expert' and, of course, they are the sort of people who wouldn't dream of claiming it for themselves.

Professional Practical Theologians?

Are Practical Theologians, then, professionals? I ought not to pose this as a closed question because, as we have seen, gradients are involved. There is certainly a body of expert knowledge – based principally around a cluster of broadly similar methods of practical theological reflection. Quite what are the boundaries that contain this expert knowledge is not quite so clear. The container

---

1 Julia Evetts *et al.*, 'Professionalization, Scientific Expertise, and Elitism: A Sociological Perspective', in K. Anders Ericsson *et al.* (eds), *The Cambridge Handbook of Expertise and Expert Performance*, Cambridge: Cambridge University Press, 2006, pp. 105–23.

2 Evetts *et al.*, 'Professionalization'. Reference is to R. Murphy, *Social Closure: The Theory of Monopolization and Exclusion*, Oxford: Clarendon Press, 1988, p. 106.

of practical theological knowledge is really quite porous, as well as being contestable.[3] To an extent this lack of rigid delimiting is useful – not least because few people remain solely within one field. Remembering that 'expert' is a relative term bestowed by peers and their authority at least acknowledged, if not formally endorsed, by the wider theological community of scholars, Practical Theology has its own gradients of prestige, privilege and power. Prestige is bestowed through academic appointments, promotions and grant-awarding bodies. The extent to which national and international associations of Practical Theology can award honour is very much in the eye of the beholder. The International Academy of Practical Theology admits only a limited number of members and requires nomination by two current members, following which an application is considered on the grounds of academic contribution to the discipline. By way of contrast, the British & Irish Association for Practical Theology admits members on the basis of their interest in the field and expressed commitment to the aims of the organization. Neither organization has market closure on Practical Theology, so prestige and privileges are correspondingly limited. The gradient of power that might mark out the field as professional is even more elusive to describe. Referees' letters to accompany job or grant applications can be significant and, in quite small networks, prove particularly influential. I think it most likely that power within the field of Practical Theology lies more in the realm of influence through individuals bestowing prestige on others. Of course, it would be foolish to imagine that Practical Theology is a wholly meritocratic discipline. The intersection with wider church politics may affect promotions and preferment – not least when these play out in academic appointments.

The diversity of interests and sometimes multiple roles of individual Practical Theologians (some might be a part-time hospital

---

3 Quite where practical, public and political theologies stop and the others begin is open to discussion. Sebastian Kim has made a case for differentiating public theology from political and liberation theologies: Sebastian Kim, *Theology in the Public Sphere: Public Theology as Catalyst for Open Debate*, London: SCM Press, 2011. Unfortunately, he chose not to attempt to do similarly with respect to Practical Theology.

chaplain, part-time parish minister, as well as undertaking research activity as a Practical Theologian) means it is very difficult, and perhaps unnecessary, to think of a distinct moral community. On the other hand, now, much more than in previous decades, Practical Theologians can avail themselves of lengthy training in both Masters and Doctoral degrees that are located within this field. If autonomy means the capacity to set its self-understanding without having to defer to another field, then Practical Theology has certainly been more self-assertive in the past 30 years. BIAPT, as an example, did not arise from a sub-group within a society of systematic theologians, but as a group of academics and practitioners (most being both) in the fields of pastoral care, chaplaincy and counselling. To state it rather bluntly, neither systematicians nor ethicists granted (nor were they invited to grant) *permission* for the development of Practical Theology. In this respect we might want to adopt the category of 'counter-elite' that sociologists of professions have proposed.[4]

I want to avoid setting up disingenuous comparisons between systematic and Practical Theology, but what we have seen of how Practical Theologians 'know we know' places us firmly within material contexts in which marginalization (perhaps through mental illness, disabilities, poverty, or sexuality – to name only a few) is significant. If counter-elites are highlighting problems that the established elites are reluctant to recognize, then Practical Theologians are most certainly helping people deal with risk. The risk may be from social stigma or the raw contingent nature of illness and accident. But the danger Practical Theologians may foreground can often be that emanating from theology itself, embodied in regressive church practices.

---

4 'In many cases single experts or small groups of experts first anticipate or perceive such a problem, make research on it, and try to initiate public discussions ... During periods of controversy the apologist experts constitute a counter-elite to established elites that are still reluctant to recognize the issue as a problem or the solutions recommended. Counter-elites play a decisive role in the generation of cultural change in modern societies and as an element of their checks and balances' (Evetts *et al.*, 'Professionalization', p. 119).

Professionalization of Practical Theology?

If, then, Practical Theology shows some signs of being a profession, there remains the matter of professionalization bound up with occupational change and control. Is there a 'professional project' within Practical Theology (remembering as we must that it is an imagined community without clear boundaries and no monopoly on this self-definition)? The development of specialist Masters and Doctoral degrees certainly points towards professionalization. In the USA – as the recent *Wiley-Blackwell Companion* demonstrates – this process is more advanced.[5] An extensive seminary system in which pastoral specialisms can flourish feeds, and is fed by, university departments. The development of a journal such as *Practical Theology* and other regional publications (e.g. South African) contribute another brick in the professional façade (although this ought not to be read as *merely* a façade).

On balance, I think we can say that some Practical Theologians inhabit an increasingly professional sphere that overlaps with other, more definitively professional, domains such as education and occupations such as chaplaincy that are further, although not wholly, down that same road. It is the professional-oriented Practical Theologians who have the greater opportunity to construct the imagined community than those favouring the less professional route. I must, however, make clear that 'less-professional' is not intended as a value-judgement upon the work of Practical Theologians who are not part of the professionalization project. Furthermore, colleagues pursuing a professionalization project are not necessarily seeking it as a totalizing and all-encompassing framework for the field. Quite what that 'third way' might look like will become more obvious as we turn to the criticism of the professionalization of pastoral care and voluntary service that have been made, respectively, by Alastair Campbell and John Reader. Seeing if these have saliency for the discipline, field or profession of Practical Theology will hopefully suggest some ways of advancing it.

---

5 Bonnie J. Miller-McLemore (ed.), *The Wiley-Blackwell Companion to Practical Theology*, Chichester: Wiley-Blackwell, 2012. I discuss this collection in detail in the second case study.

Transcending professionalism

Almost 30 years ago Alastair Campbell, then still at the University of Edinburgh, contributed to the discussion of the limits of professionalism in pastoral care. Our theme of Practical Theology as critical reflection on practice is much wider than this, but revisiting the debate from a rather different angle is useful. Campbell boils down the conflict of the 1970s into two perspectives, embodied in the works of Howard Clinebell in the USA and Robert Lambourne in the UK:

> For Clinebell the notion of expertise remains normative: for Lambourne it is precisely the use of this norm which creates the danger. Clinebell wants the expert to teach the laity: Lambourne wants to mobilize the laity so that they can challenge the narrowness of vision of the experts ... In the last analysis, the difference may be seen as between a writer who views *care* from the perspective of *counselling* and one who views *counselling* from the perspective of *care*.[6]

I do not suggest that we merely substitute expert practical theological reflection for *counselling* and lay practical theological reflection for *care* in order to re-run the debate. Pastoral care is a much more recognizable practice among non-experts than is practical theological reflection. The social (dare we say professional) contexts are markedly different from those of clinical pastoral education where ministers were, in many versions of the US model, trained in pastoral counselling through field placements in hospitals. Nevertheless, there are some similarities for our purposes here.

Campbell helps us to see the implications of expertise being set as normative by asking questions of 'lack of mutuality; maldistribution of influence and power; intellectualism; neglect of the communal dimension; and resistance to radical change'.[7]

---

6 Alistair V. Campbell, *Paid to Care? The Limits of Professionalism in Pastoral Care*, London: SPCK, 1985, p. 40.

7 Campbell, *Paid*, p. 40.

Lack of mutuality

Churches have a strange attitude to people's areas of professional expertise. A teacher is presumed to be cannon fodder for children's work. A musician is expected to contribute to the worship ministry. An accountant will be dragooned into treasurership or at least sitting on the finance committee. A manual labourer will be first in line for janitorial duties. Beyond those skills that map directly to congregational activities, the Church generally sees professional expertise as irrelevant. When it comes to practical theological reflection, the picture ought to be wholly different. The movement within the cycle of reflection that analyses a practice from sociological, cultural, psychological, historical, economic or any other discipline demands experienced insight. Most often, as Lartey has pointed out, academic Practical Theologians are not as well-versed in the knowledge-base and, even more importantly, the nuances of other fields than they are in theology. His admirably workable solution in the absence of collaboration between academics from a number of fields is to adopt a multi-perspectival position.[8] Funding constraints, accessibility to colleagues willing to be associated with Practical Theology and the brute shortage of time mean this is the best possible approach for most Practical Theologians in academic settings.[9]

The vast resource of experts in their own field among the members of Christian churches remains to be mined to anything like the extent that could be possible. Practical Theologians do worry that we work too often in ways that appear disconnected from the communities of Christian faith. Conversely, highly intelligent and knowledge people worship in contexts that, whether intentionally or not, bracket out their professional expertise. Practical Theology holds every possibility for a sociologist in St Mungo's Parish Church to deploy her expertise in a piece of reflective research.

---

8 Emmanuel Lartey, 'Practical Theology as a Theological Form', in James Woodward and Stephen Pattison (eds), *The Blackwell Reader in Pastoral and Practical Theology*, Oxford: Blackwell, 2000 [1996], p. 132.

9 Colleagues from other disciplines have to weigh up any loss of prestige that interdisciplinary work with theologians might bring them within their professional context.

This need not be under the auspices of her academic employer as a full-blown project, but could well see her working for a short, concise exercise alongside a Practical Theologian who would most likely be a member of another congregation. The same could be said of an economist at City Baptist Church or an urban geographer who worships at the Roman Catholic cathedral.

Mutuality could be expressed by drawing on available expertise or by first identifying the experts around whom a collaborative piece of practical theological work could be initiated. Why shouldn't someone with extensive experience of the power distribution industry be offered the opportunity to facilitate practical theological reflection on environmental impact or electricity costs in their wider area? Naturally, possible conflicts of interest and commercial confidentiality need to be addressed, but such challenges can be tackled.

As much as Masters and Doctoral dissertations advance the discipline, the exigencies of academic awards requires identifiably *individual* work; a person, not a team, gets a PhD. Too much focus on this dimension of professionalization will be at the cost of realizing the potential of informal projects. These need be no less rigorous, but be different in being truly interdisciplinary, *drawing on the expertise of people already in the pews*.

Maldistribution of influence and power

Campbell was well aware of the tendency of professionals to accumulate power. This, he saw, tends to be replicated in church where there is a 'middle class captivity' that dominates the helping roles.[10] As a consequence, pastoral care issues become the issues of that well-educated middle class at the expense of the less-educated and possibly less-articulate members of the congregation.[11] Furthermore, 'the insights of the poor and lowly are lost'.[12] In terms of Practical Theology I think this is an equally pressing challenge.

---

10 Campbell, *Paid*, p. 44.

11 Being ignored or silenced as a minority does not mean one is potentially less articulate than those given, or taking, a voice.

12 Campbell, *Paid*, p. 45.

Associations such as BIAPT struggle to negotiate the interests, ethos and needs of practitioners and academics. Professionalizing the discipline results in the title 'Practical Theologian' being kept for those within the guild. That's all well and good for medicine or law (perhaps), but the related factors of educational attainment and social class pose uncomfortable questions for Practical Theology.

By virtue of both higher education and the professions in which we make a living, Practical Theologians are predominantly, if not exclusively, middle class. I appreciate that this is a blunt social category given the more sophisticated models now in operation.[13] However, we share a common enough sense of what 'middle class' represents. Now, broadly speaking, Practical Theologians are little different, demographically speaking, from the Christian Church in the UK, and most certainly are typical of the movers and shakers in all denominations and most Christian organizations.

The complexity of models of practical theological reflection – a necessity in developing robust and defensible methodologies – reinforces professionalization, but with the consequence that it is reserved for certain sectors of the Christian community. Again, there are exceptions that prove the rule,[14] but the umbrella of Practical Theology seems to shelter a rather limited range of people reflecting on their experiences using something akin to a cycle of reflection.[15] This is where our awareness of Practical Theology as an *imagined community* is vital. My metaphor of an umbrella is not to be taken as a statement that those beyond its coverage are not doing, or not entitled to call what they are doing, 'Practical Theology'. There is no need for them so to do. My point is simply that 'Practical Theology' in this imagined community sense is

13 Mike Savage *et al.*, 'A New Model of Social Class? Findings from the BBC's Great British Class Survey Experiment', *Sociology* 47.2 (2013), pp. 219–50.

14 Here I'm thinking about the late Marcella Althaus-Reid's work with women in Dundee, Urban Priority Area congregational development, and other urban theology movements – as well as some contextual Bible studies.

15 I fully accept that this is equally a criticism of my case study of a group discussing Scottish Independence. I can only plead the constraints of time and contacts in my defence.

turning out to be worryingly homogeneous – at least as regards social class, and particularly educational attainment. This is not a criticism of BIAPT or other associations for they cannot be – and ought not attempt to be – totalizing movements that embrace, smother or otherwise validate Practical Theology as a whole. Perish the thought! Rather, I observe a phenomenon all too common in British (and perhaps other national contexts) Christianity: the middle-class 'market closure'.

I live in a regenerated area of Edinburgh previously known for significant deprivation. Among the many home owners live people in houses rented by associations. Our area can support a new Tesco Metro alongside Lidl and Londis. Readers familiar with the British retail-scape will appreciate the economic profile of low-cost super-markets. I have no connections with the two local parish churches that once served exclusively working-class and unemployed communities. I overhear conversations in the queue at Londis that strongly suggest that those people are unable to work and are reliant on benefits. To be honest, the contrast with my neighbourhood and the environs of St Andrews, where I teach at the university with its well-known image, disturbs me – but not enough. What on earth could practical theological reflection mean for Christians with poor educational achievement and reliant on the minimum wage and benefits? I don't suggest I have a simple answer, but perhaps our antennae towards the distribution of power that is developed in our liberationist models of reflection need to twitch more than a little towards our own discipline.

Intellectualism

The captivity that Campbell finds here is not that of the intellectual grasp of, and development of, a complex body of knowledge that is inimical to a professional stance. Rather, he challenges the way in which intellectual attainment is made 'an ideal for all …[in which] only those who *know* can love God and neighbour'.[16] Practical Theologians exploring the experience of people with intellectual

---

16 Campbell, *Paid*, p. 45.

impairments (whether through cognitive development or forms of dementia) have been bringing this to our attention with exceptional clarity in recent years.[17] They have faced what it means to listen for the limited or fragmentary witness of people who are unable to articulate their experience in words or communicable gestures. As much as has been possible, these researchers have been involving people with impairments as participants and not simply as objects of study. If we set such research to one side I do wonder if Campbell's criticism of intellectualism in pastoral care does not also impact upon Practical Theology.

Exploring the maldistribution of power we touched on this, but low educational achievement is not synonymous with intellectual capacity; systemic barriers as well as personal circumstances can preclude intelligent people from securing the qualifications of which they are capable. Intellectualism is a rather different charge.

I think Practical Theology comes off rather better here than in the previous criticisms. Thanks largely to feminist ways of knowing, embodiment and creative forms of expression have a substantial profile within the discipline.[18] However, the primary mode of communicating practical theological reflection remains cognitive and discursive; the product in the form of a report uses words – with the occasional image in support. Again, the requirements of universities prevail – and understandably so – although portfolio work is possible.[19] It seems to me that there are at least two dimensions here. One covers the ways in which practical theological reflection takes place; another revolves around how the results of that reflection are not so much implemented but presented to outsiders.

Walton, Ward and Graham have identified seven methods of reflection in a practical theological mode. Journalling and cre-

---

17 Most notably, John Swinton, *Dementia: Living in the Memories of God*, London: SCM Press, 2012.

18 For example, Jan Berry, *Ritual Making Women: Shaping Rites for Changing Lives*, London: Equinox, 2009; Elaine Graham and Margaret Halsey (eds), *Life Cycles: Women and Pastoral Care*, London: SPCK, 1993; Heather Walton, *Imagining Theology: Women, Writing, and God*, London: T. & T. Clark, 2007.

19 As is the case in, for example, the Professional Doctorate in Practical Theology offered by a consortium of universities in the UK.

ative writing are significant for more than reflection on our interior life ('theology by heart'). Telling stories ('speaking in parables') is an oral practice (although sometimes relying on writing), but one in which we must take care over the dominant metaphors we deploy.[20] Other methods, such as 'telling God's story' or corporate theological reflection, do tip rather towards text – again because of the communicative, if not also regulative, aspects; sharing reflection and inducting others into its benefits remains wedded to the written word.

Practising faith in a different way, what might be called witness through actions, is built into all models of practical theological reflection. The 'response' box on any diagram does not mean 'writing a report' (although that is often required to evidence the process – rather like having to show your workings in solving a maths problem). As I say, our focus on practice and embodied ways of knowing and relating to others mitigates against the charge of intellectualism. Finding ways to articulate our findings in forms other than standard reports remains a challenge.

Neglect of communal dimension

Here Campbell picked up Lambourne's concern that professionalization of pastoral care into the form of pastoral counselling was individualizing, and thus limiting, the scope of the field: 'urban renewal, minority rights, peace movements and other moral concerns espoused by Christians have not found any place in the dominant "clinical" model of pastoral care'.[21] Practical Theology most certainly has the social and often systemic political dimensions built into the models of critical reflection. But that is not quite the point of bringing Campbell's criticism across to this field. We've envisaged a communal dimension earlier in the involvement of Christians with professional expertise in informal (as distinct from academically driven) reflection. If I am correct with my notion of

---

20 Elaine Graham *et al.*, *Theological Reflection: Methods*, London: SCM Press, 2005, p. 73.

21 Campbell, *Paid*, p. 47.

critical discipleship, then finding ways of re-presenting regular and long-established Christian practices as opportunities for this sort of reflection seems important.

As just one small example, in what ways might corporate intercession during Sunday worship be recast from a critical discipleship practical theological perspective? The choice of what and who to pray for is never innocent and sometimes irritating. Learning how to attend to the others queuing for Holy Communion might be another opportunity. Practical theological reflection has not made much of its communal potential beyond involving a few people in a research project.

Resistance to social change

Campbell turns to the social function of professions who, as we have seen, institutionalize expertise for communities that are too large for everyone to personally validate another person's skills. A professional group needs to present a united front to the public and so is inherently conservative – preserving the relationship the group has been able to establish with the non-expert public.[22] Campbell argues that professional accreditation makes pastoral counsellors less likely to be critical of their position.[23] Now, as there is no similar move towards formal recognition or accreditation of Practical Theologians, there is no position to maintain. Perhaps because so many Practical Theologians are already working on the margins of their denomination, institution or university, they are people for whom social change is an objective. It is easier to be (or at least pose as) radical when you have relatively little to lose in terms of prestige or power.

---

22 Campbell, *Paid*, p. 47.
23 Campbell, *Paid*, p. 47.

Critical professionalism

As a way forward for pastoral care and counselling in the 1980s, Campbell argued for the 'transcendence of professionalism'.[24] His point was that while much is gained in the professionalization of pastoral care – not least in the greater safety for vulnerable clients – 'the spontaneity and the simplicity that characterize love' was in danger of being lost.[25] It is in the transcendence, not abandonment, of professionalism that he believed the Christian vision might be effectively expressed:

> The realism, skill and relative detachment of the professional helper, who is 'paid to care', are important features of any caring ministry. They must, however, be complemented by the simplicity, fresh vision and hopefulness of people who, having known love, wish to share it.[26]

Some 20 years later John Reader was to make a similar point about Christian voluntary social agencies, albeit with a greater immediate concern for what was rapidly being lost:

> Who am I though as just one human being relating to another in this exchange? My understanding of the Christian tradition is that it encourages an open or messianic approach to identity. I do not yet know who I am or who I might become within that divine economy which I call the Kingdom of God. My relationships with others therefore have to retain a high degree of uncertainty, spontaneity and unpredictability in order for God to work through me for good. I am not in control of this process nor should I imagine that I could be. Yet much of what we experience now through the professionalization of voluntary activity is precisely about retaining control through the setting of clear and identifiable boundaries. I know exactly who I am and what I have to offer in this carefully defined situation and I equally know who

---

24 Campbell, *Paid*, p. 73.
25 Campbell, *Paid*, p. 4.
26 Campbell, *Paid*, p. 34.

you are and what your problem is and therefore what resources I can offer, hence I can set limits to the exchange and find reasons to withdraw. There can be no justification for withdrawal from the relationship according to the example of Christ though.[27]

Reader recognized that expectations placed upon Christian charitable organizations to achieve targets and adopt evaluation criteria from the professional world can lead to an unchristian over-protection of the boundaries of the self of the carer and, in some cases, withdrawal (or not offering) of support to those whose actions adversely impact upon 'success' rates. We could add to concerns over professionalization the challenges facing healthcare chaplains working in task-oriented, evidence-based contexts, where only particular skills and competencies are valued, at the expense of attributes nurtured in contemplation and meditation.[28]

Practical Theologians live in the tension between the increasing sophistication of practical theological method that requires these tools to be in the hands of experts and the need to both value and facilitate the contribution of lay (in the sense of non-expert) Practical Theologians.[29] Something akin to Campbell's notion of a transcendence of professionalism may be required. This is not a rejection of professional Practical Theology, but an enhancement of it.

---

27 John Reader, 'The Professionalisation of Voluntary Activity', *Contact* 144 (2004), p. 21.

28 Mark Clayton, 'Contemplative Chaplaincy? A View from a Children's Hospice', *Practical Theology* 6.1 (2013).

29 The critical rigour, methodological awareness and writing style appropriate to an academic journal such as *Practical Theology* cannot be expected of lay contributors. For this reason, *Practical Theology* created two separate categories of writing: theological reflection and soapbox but, despite effort, it has proved to be difficult to secure contributions for these different modes of communication. One notable exception within the regular articles category is an autobiographical piece written from within the autistic spectrum: Christopher Barber, 'On Connectedness: Spirituality on the Autistic Spectrum', *Practical Theology* 4.2 (2011), pp. 201–11. As a soapbox contribution, see a personal perspective on chaplaincy from one who has previously written in the genre of sociology: Ruth Ann Jolly, 'Chaplaincy Works', *Practical Theology* 4.3 (2011), pp. 359–61.

One step towards laicizing Practical Theology is in the more intentional involvement of people in churches who have, through their own professional lives, significant levels of expert knowledge in, for example, economics, literature, business or law.[30] A different step is to articulate Practical Theology as a means towards *critical discipleship*. This is not to replace programmes that concentrate on the interior life and what normally is bracketed as 'spirituality'. Neither ought we to deny a place for doctrinal learning and induction in the practices of prayer and worship (as traditionally understood). If Practical Theology is to make the most of its professionalization without succumbing to the perils of such a project, we need to be much more deliberate in making the tried and tested methods of reflection *on the whole of everyday life* more accessible to non-expert Christian people. Our everyday lives include but are not limited to the domestic sphere, so no dimension of what people do can be off-limits for practical theological reflection. If the future could lie in this direction, we need to ask, given the tendency towards middle-class closure, quite how radical such a project needs to be.

---

30 Laicization is not meant here in the sense of someone leaving holy orders, but as a way of referring to the widening of access to Practical Theology as a field, so that it is not confined within a professional caste.

6

A Passport to the Future

Malcolm X said, 'Education is our passport to the future, for tomorrow belongs to the people who prepare for it today.'[1] I entirely agree, and far more significant voices than mine have taken a similar approach. For Paulo Freire the key to breaking cycles of poverty and violence lay in liberating education.[2] His influence on how Groome developed his model of Shared Praxis is obvious and clearly acknowledged.[3] I wonder if we can, at least for our limited purposes, envisage Practical Theology as properly the core of the education of Christian people to be critical disciples – vigorous social commentators and participants in God's beautiful and broken world? It might seem presumptuous, but what if *Practical Theology is our passport to the future*? The models of theological reflection that we make more accessible to non-experts in order that together we fulfil the calling to be critical disciples appear to be dangerous. Thinking critically threatens the status quo – whether at work, rest or play (and how one's Christian discipleship is distributed across those three categories is likely more complex and fascinating than it might at first appear). But, quite how threatening? To what extent are Practical Theologians genuinely a 'counter-elite'? If Practical

---

1 Malcolm X, 'Speech at the Founding Rally of the Organization of Afro-American Unity, Given at Harlem 28th June 1964', *By Any Means Necessary: Speeches, Interviews, and a Letter by Malcolm X*, New York: Pathfinder Press, 1970.

2 Paulo Freire, *Pedagogy of the Oppressed*, London: Penguin Books, 1970.

3 Thomas H. Groome, 'Religious Knowing: Still Looking for That Tree', *Religious Education* 92.2 (1997), p. 222; *Sharing Faith: A Comprehensive Approach to Religious Education and Pastoral Ministry: The Way of Shared Praxis*, Eugene, OR: Wipf and Stock, 1998, p. 184.

Theology is to be more accessible, then *what sort of* Practical Theology ought that to be?

Don't just add women or the poor and stir

A little over 25 years ago Rebecca Chopp posed a similar question about the developments in Practical Theology at that time. The focus then was on finding ways of correlating meaning and truth from Christian theology with that of contemporary social, political, cultural and scientific understanding.[4] Practical Theology would thus be a public theology – in the sense that its arguments are 'available in principle to any attentive, intelligent, rational and responsible human being'.[5] By appealing to the principles of reason correlation was to be possible over abstract, metaphysical questions. More specific claims to truth could be engaged through the idea of classic works – in literature or art – alongside which the Bible is another classic. At its most concrete this process involved Practical Theology offering and examining others' models of how humans are transformed – giving particular attention to where there are distortions in those models.[6] This correlation was intended to be two-way; religion (specifically Christian faith) would be responsive to other understandings which, in turn, would be willing to refine their ideas in the light of specifically Christian critique. However, Chopp was quite right to observe that this is a theological position that 'posits an underlying unity between individuals and tradition, and believes that it can reconcile, through understanding, human experience to reality'.[7]

Chopp was not out to dismiss totally this way of conceptualizing theology (it is properly identified as the 'liberal project'), but she

4 David Tracy, 'The Foundations of Practical Theology', in Don S. Browning (ed.), *Practical Theology: The Emerging Field in Theology, Church and World*, San Francisco: Harper & Row, 1983.

5 Tracy, 'Foundations', p. 66.

6 Tracy, 'Foundations', pp. 77–8.

7 Rebecca S. Chopp, 'Practical Theology and Liberation', in Lewis S. Mudge and James N. Poling (eds), *Formation and Reflection: The Promise of Practical Theology*, Philadelphia: Fortress Press, 1987, p. 120.

was concerned that such a model and, consequently, discussions, writings and influence – particularly upon the Church – was obscuring vital issues. In stark terms, Chopp found that liberal revised correlational Practical Theology (as espoused by Tracy) hid the ways in which the Church makes itself compliant with middle-class life and values.[8]

Chopp turned to Liberation Theology for a corrective that attends much more explicitly to the voices of those ignored, misrepresented, forgotten or oppressed by Liberal Theology and liberal societies. Such a shift is not simply tinkering with liberal Practical Theology but bearing down on it with a radically different way of acting and thinking.[9] Just as Feminist Theologians were *not* suggesting an 'add woman and stir' sweetening, as it were, of Christian faith-practice, neither was Chopp blind to the radical critique she was making. To incorporate Liberation Theology into Practical Theology was not, metaphorically speaking, dissolving a new substance into the liquid of the liberal project that would change its flavour. Rather, if I might put it rather clumsily, the result would be changing Practical Theology from a liquid to an axe. As Chopp put it:

> Liberation theologians ask different questions, consider different human experiences and existences, and most of all, experience Christianity in a very different way than liberal theologians are able to conceive of or reflect upon.[10]

It is important to revisit this shift in Practical Theology, because it pushes us today to be sure we really know what Practical Theology is *for*. Chopp, in 1987, contrasted the questions about

---

8 Chopp, 'Practical', p. 120. Chopp actually refers to Johannes Baptist Metz's argument about the Church and bourgeois existence: see Johannes Baptist Metz, *Faith in History and Society: Toward a Practical Fundamental Theology*, trans. David Smith, New York: Seabury Press, 1980; *The Emergent Church: The Future of Christianity in a Post-Bourgeois World*, trans. Peter Mann, New York: Crossroad, 1981.

9 The singular 'way' is important here in order to keep thinking and acting together conceptually.

10 Chopp, 'Practical', p. 122.

political representation, hunger and life itself that were posed by people rendered largely 'nonpersons' in the liberal (both theological and public) framework with those of bourgeois Christians who wanted to know how to retain religious belief in a secular world and how that belief might be properly guarded as private. Human experience could no longer be evaluated against the plumb line of middle-class, liberal existence (presented as if it were the norm or common human experience). Nor could the liberal idea of rationality as the proper – i.e. universal – only valid way of knowing be protected.[11] Theology could not be a way of defending religious belief; it had to become, for Chopp, a way of radical action-critique of political and social structures that gave voice to 'nonpersons'.

What, then, in 2014 is Practical Theology *for*? Many of us would like to think that it is for transformed practices within the Church and, through informed social comment and democratic persuasion, a contribution to establishing structures, policies and encounters that contribute to people's flourishing. However, I do not believe we can take that for granted – even as an objective – let alone as actual, rubber-hitting-the-road change. Liberation Theology has been criticized for losing its way in the last few years – not least since the demolition of the Berlin Wall and the supposed victory of capitalism and the defeat of socialism. We might turn those criticisms to the household of Practical Theology and see if we might have lost – or perhaps be in danger of losing – our way.

If it were not for the tragic cost of human life and well-being, it strikes me as amusing how relatively quickly one period's 'radicals' become closely connected with, and invested in, the establishment status quo.[12] The British Labour Party is so thoroughly 'establishment' in a way that its socialist forebears among the working class might well have seen, in their day, as a gross betrayal. Baptists, once living dangerously as roughish separatists from an intrusive state, are now remarkably mainstream, collaborating in government-sponsored welfare projects. No one supporting the right of women in the UK to vote is viewed as in the least bit radical; that particular

---

11 Chopp, 'Practical', p. 130.

12 We will discuss the importance of reclaiming terms such as 'radical' later.

battle is done and dusted. Times change and what was once contentious, beyond the pale, or downright subversive is now almost
universally accepted as 'simply how it always ought to have been'.
We are thankful for this in so many ways but one consequence is
that radicals cannot rest on their laurels.

More concerning, even tragic, are the radical projects that
dissipate not because of fulfilled objectives, but through the attri-
tion arising when small improvements are achieved but no more.
Being radical in name only is a sad condition, although it may be
tempered by the smothering embrace of the establishment who
has brought you in from the cold or, to put it rather differently,
distracted you with a few tidbits while neutering you. Theological
movements are not exempt from such developments – although
such an ignominious end is by no means inevitable. We have seen
the close affinity, in some respects, between Liberation Theology
and Practical Theology. Ivan Petrella has been critical of Liberation Theology on a number of counts and, given our partly shared
history as forms of reflection, it will do no harm, and hopefully
some good, to see to what extent Petrella's contentions also apply
to Practical Theology.

Beyond the future

Petrella's calling of Liberation Theology to account is contained
in his companion texts, *The Future of Liberation Theology* and
Beyond Liberation Theology.[13] Admittedly polemical, his analysis
bears serious consideration. In a nutshell he finds that Liberation
Theology fails to place historical projects at the heart of its current
self-understanding. This is not simply then a plea for more activ-
ism, but a call to see both concrete action and the social sciences
as integral to constructive projects. Petrella is arguing thus against
any bifurcation of the reign of God and politics:

---

13 Ivan Petrella, *The Future of Liberation Theology: An Argument and
Manifesto*, London: SCM Press, 2006, and *Beyond Liberation Theology: A
Polemic*, London: SCM Press, 2008.

my argument denies the theology/sociopolitical analysis split in two ways: first, by collapsing the distinction between the theological and the political and insisting on the development of what could be called the material component of liberation theology's categories. Within my scheme, 'the preferential option for the poor' and 'liberation' are not just values by which the theologian judges society. They are to be developed as alternative social forms: that is, political, economic and social institutions that can be enacted at society's many levels ... Second, the split is refuted by remembering that liberation theology's goal is not to talk about liberation, but concrete liberation itself.[14]

His is not an uncritical acceptance of any or all social scientific theories for the task of the Liberation Theologian includes unmasking the implicit theologies of the social sciences.

The social sciences are, for Petrella, a source of discovering what the reign of God means in deeply particular contexts with a considerable degree of specificity. Petrella's is not the world of retreat to theological generalities out of a fear of being poorly informed and inadvertently prescriptive. The cost of such reticence, in his opinion, has been a sickness in Liberation Theology that has meant it has lost sight of the actual conditions of people's poverty that it at first set out to address. In *Beyond Liberation Theology* Petrella draws attention to the material context in which Liberation Theologians – particularly those in the USA – are writing. He finds that they have been 'unable to face the spread of zones of abandonment'.[15] This, he argues, is due to the way many, especially US, Liberation Theologians have come to see the world. For Liberation Theology to be restored to health Petrella argues that four conditions must be addressed: monochromatism, amnesia, gigantism and naiveté.[16] We need now to look at these challenges in more detail before we can use them to evaluate Practical Theology in our second case study.

---

14 Petrella, *Future*, p. 39.
15 Petrella, *Beyond*, p. 82.
16 Petrella, *Beyond*, p. 105.

Monochromatism

Petrella is writing specifically with Liberation Theology in the USA in mind and he focuses particularly on discussions within black Liberation Theology. On the one hand, there are black theologies such as the early work of James Cone that deploy 'black' as a way of talking about all forms of oppression – regardless of one's actual skin colour. On the other, is a perspective such as that of Gayraud Wilmore who wants to draw exclusively on black theological resources such as 'mythology, folk lore and ethical norms'.[17] Here the experience of being black is not transferable to the extent that the expert analyses of non-black social scientists and theologians is not admissible. In Petrella's opinion such a stance severely limits the relevance of black Liberation Theology for advancing the actual liberation of poor (black) people in the USA.[18]

Amnesia

For Petrella, amnesia is a debilitating condition seen when theologians 'forget the problems they seek to tackle and the goals they want to pursue'.[19] He identifies three steps that begin with a stress on the alleviating of poverty, but slide into a theological construction that forgets the primary goal of tackling poverty and is replaced by 'the cultural advancement of a particular ethnic group'.[20] Petrella's first example is Maria Pilar Aquino, a Latina Feminist Theologian, who analyses the plight of Latina first in terms of global poverty and social exclusion; then, more specifically in the USA, with reference to the rates of poverty of children, minorities and families headed by women; and, thirdly, Aquino is exercised over the exclusion of Latina women from authorized and recognized theological activity. Petrella finds amnesia in the order in which Aquino sets

---

17 Gayraud S. Wilmore, *Black Theology and Black Radicalism: An Interpretation of the Religious History of Afro-American People*, Maryknoll, NY: Orbis Books, 1983, p. 237. Quoted in Petrella, *Beyond*, p. 86.

18 Petrella, *Beyond*, p. 92.

19 Petrella, *Beyond*, p. 93.

20 Petrella, *Beyond*, p. 93.

out the tasks of a Latina Feminist Theology. He expects to see a critique of economic conditions at the top of the list of tasks, but instead he finds it fourth in Aquino's sequence. It is 'access to theological education and intellectual construction' that comes first.[21] Petrella believes this to be a 'class choice' in which 'helping people become theologians is given priority over helping people lift themselves from social misery'.[22] Petrella's conclusion is that while this is an important task, Aquino demonstrates forgetfulness of the endemic poverty of most Latinas: 'What really has priority is the inclusion of Latinas into the United States' mainstream.'[23]

As with each of his criticisms, it is not my aim here to determine the extent to which he is correct about his selected examples in particular or Liberation Theology as a whole. Rather, I want to take such challenges and see what saliency they have for Practical Theology as we encounter and practise it today.

Gigantism

Gigantism is the flip-side of amnesia, because material poverty is kept firmly in focus, but the Liberation Theologian is paralysed by the immensity of the overbearing power believed to be embedded in capitalist inequality. The capitalist system, so the gigantist argument goes, holds all the world in its grip, permitting the development of a few countries at the expense of the exploitation of the many. Petrella finds this baldly stated in Gustavo Gutiérrez's classic texts.[24] Gutiérrez, in Petrella's view, faces 'an awesome enemy'; 'capitalism necessarily produces underdevelopment, this

---

21 Petrella, *Beyond*, p. 95. Petrella's reference is to Maria Pilar Aquino, 'Latina Feminist Theology: Central Features', in Maria Pilar Aquino *et al.* (eds), *A Reader in Latina Feminist Theology: Religion and Justice*, Austin, TX: University of Texas Press, 2002.

22 Petrella, *Beyond*, p. 95.

23 Petrella, *Beyond*, p. 96.

24 Gustavo Gutiérrez, *A Theology of Liberation*, London: SCM Press, 2001 [1974], and *Praxis De Liberacíon Y Fe Cristianan*, Madrid: Zero, 1974. See Petrella, *Beyond*, p. 102.

necessity is part of capitalism's very definition'.[25] Other Liberation Theologians conceive of their foe in similar terms, according to Petrella. Pablo Richard is presented as treating globalization in the same 'all-encompassing' and 'inherently exploitative' terms.[26]

Naiveté

Petrella finds that a naïve response often occurs as a consequence of monochromatism, amnesia or gigantism. A Liberation Theologian's naiveté is exposed when he tries to outline specific courses of action – which might be reform and/or resistance. 'At this point worldly and sophisticated theologians, stricken by naiveté, suddenly become ingenuous, credulous and succumb to wishful thinking and/or poetic rapture in which rhetoric is pumped up to mask an absence of ideas.'[27] The sort of soaring rhetoric he has in mind occurs, in Petrella's evaluation, in the work of womanist theologian Emilie Townes: 'The society that is part of the new Jerusalem respects and cares for the young and the elderly. It is a society that is rich in diversity ... that does not dwell on sexual orientation or life-style.'[28]

Petrella's proposals

Petrella makes a number of proposals that he believes could be productive for Liberation Theology – and I think raise further interesting challenges. He picks up Barth's aphorism against becoming accustomed to the unimaginable. Outrage ought, then,

---

25 Petrella, *Beyond*, p. 102.

26 Petrella, *Beyond*, p. 103. Petrella is referring specifically to Pablo Richard, 'Teología De La Solidaridad En El Contexto Actual De Economía Neoliberal De Mercado', in Franz Hinkelammert (ed.), *El Huracán De La Globalización*, San José, Costa Rica: DEI, 1999.

27 Petrella, *Beyond*, p. 105.

28 Emilie M. Townes, 'Living in the New Jerusalem: The Rhetoric and Movement of Liberation in the House of Evil', in Emilie M. Townes (ed.), *A Troubling in My Soul: Womanist Perspectives on Evil and Suffering*, Maryknoll, NY: Orbis, 2002, p. 89. Quoted in Petrella, *Beyond*, p. 107.

to be nurtured in order that we remember that 'horror is not the exception but the rule'.[29] For Petrella, Liberation Theology has to broaden its scope beyond that of the Church, because, despite its own assertions to be 'secular', there are practices and ways of making meaning in the world that are acutely dangerous for the people's flourishing:

> Today ... the most dangerous religions and theologies, those that affect the life chances of the greatest number of people, are not found in churches or the traditionally religious sphere, but outside of it, in what is mistakenly understood as the secular world.[30]

The systemic hindrances to people's flourishing are throughout the world and not confined to what was traditionally defined as the Third World. This is the mistake that Petrella believes belies the ineffectiveness of US liberation theologies. They are unable to see that *within* the USA the 'Third World' issues are highly pertinent for vast numbers of marginalized and impoverished people. Effective theologies will need to consider themselves, says Petrella, as 'Third/Two-Thirds World Theologies'.[31] International boundaries or outdated economic divisions of development are not respected by inequality, injustice and oppression.

Liberation Theologians also have to reject being categorized as 'contextual theologies' because this 'takes the edge off their critique'.[32] At first sight this seems rather innocuous until we appreciate that Petrella is aware of the ways in which dominant theological voices can cover up the very radical difference between so-called 'conversation partners'; some (usually the dominant) are interested in interpretation of transcendence, while Liberation Theology is about the construction of transcendence, not being in conversation but in conflict for material betterment of particular people.[33]

---

29 Petrella, *Beyond*, p. 124.
30 Petrella, *Beyond*, p. 128.
31 Petrella, *Beyond*, p. 128.
32 Petrella, *Beyond*, p. 132.
33 Petrella, *Beyond*, p. 133. Petrella is here openly following Manuel Mejido, 'Beyond the Postmodern Condition, or the Turn toward Psycho-

Such objectives put Liberation Theology in a close – even, argues Petrella, an *integral* – relationship to the social sciences. It is not going to be theology that provides the tools for getting to the causes of, for example, rates of black incarceration, and enables construction of political, social or other forms of concrete response.[34] At the same time, the social sciences 'are the means to unmask the false neutrality of theological concepts by working out their political, economic, and social implications'.[35] In Petrella's sights are not only theologies of the liberal project, but racial and ethnic liberation theologies. The core question is thus: 'what makes this theology liberative to the materially poor?'[36]

This fundamental reclamation of liberation theologies had been opened up by Petrella in his earlier work, *Future of Liberation Theology*:

> Thus for liberation theology the construction of historical projects should not be a secondary moment in the theological tasks, coming after the clarification of our theological concepts, but rather must become a central means by which those concepts are clarified, given analytical rigor [sic] and understood.[37]

As a way out of the impasse of gigantism and its consequent paralysis, Petrella developed links between Liberation Theology and Robert Unger's social theory towards 'the deepening of democracy and the expansion of economic opportunity'.[38] Unger's notion of 'alternative pluralisms' via 'step-by-step construction of alternative political and economic institutions' enabled Petrella to hold out an alternative:

> Neither capitalism nor society forms a coherent and systemic whole waiting to be toppled and replaced by another whole.

---

analysis', in Ivan Petralla (ed.), *Latin American Liberation Theology: The Next Generation*, Maryknoll, NY: Orbis Books, 2005, pp. 119–46.

34 Petrella, *Beyond*, p. 136.
35 Petrella, *Beyond*, p. 136.
36 Petrella, *Beyond*, p. 141.
37 Petrella, *Future*, p. 37.
38 Petrella, *Future*, p. 93.

Society has no a priori foundation and remains constantly constructed, deconstructed and reconstructed through a variety of
discursive and political struggles.[39]

Such construction, deconstruction and reconstruction would, in
Petrella's view, benefit from a liberation theological contribution,
but 'liberation' would require to be disentangled from 'Liberation Theology'. Experts in 'non-theological' fields would work in
their respective institutions and structures in a quite unorthodox
manner: 'The liberation theologian must operate undercover as an
economist or legal theorist and work from within to transform the
discipline's presuppositions.'[40] Given Petrella's redrawing of the
boundaries of 'theological' through his view that 'the social sciences are the places where God's promise of life is realized', such
work is not 'non-theological' at all but deeply theological.[41] This
is a crucial step in understanding, and later redirecting, Petrella's
critique, because it can be difficult to break out of the framework
that limits 'theological' to the traditional areas of Christian doctrine. It is only fair to acknowledge Petrella's view of God and
God's activity is itself radical – he identifies as an agnostic.[42] Yet if
one can grasp that the world is potentially sacramental to us – the
material encounters in which God can make Godself known to us
– then perhaps Petrella's is not so large a step to take.[43]

Petrella's target has been US liberation theologies. We can
extend the radical critique by turning to that offered against new
economic, military and cultural imperialism, in the postcolonial
contribution of Míguez, Rieger and Sung.

---

39 Petrella, *Future*, p. 99.

40 Petrella, *Beyond*, p. 148.

41 Petrella, *Beyond*, p. 135; Petrella, *Future*, p. 33.

42 Sociedad, 'Sólo Le Pido Adios' http://edant.clarin.com/diario/
2006/04/02/sociedad/s-01169625.htm. See also Mario Aguilar, *The History
and Politics of Latin American Theology – Volume 2*, London: SCM Press,
2008, p. 168.

43 For my own take on the potential sacramentality of the world, see
Eric Stoddart, 'Spirituality and Citizenship: Sacramentality in a Parable',
Theological Studies 68 (2007), pp. 761–79.

Beyond Empire

Néstor Míguez, like Petrella, is an Argentinian, but, unlike Petrella, he remains located in Latin America – in Buenos Aires. Joerg Rieger, originally from Germany, now teaches in Perkins School of Theology in Dallas, Texas. Jung Mo Sung was born in South Korea, but has lived in Brazil for almost 40 years. Together, these three men have authored *Beyond the Spirit of Empire*. Their key point for my discussion is that Empire affects the subjectivity of those whom it designates in whatever forms: good, bad, outsider, etc. One effect of this subjectivity is that Empire is then (in its form of capitalism) the only show in town. What is needed is a radical critique of how people are being shaped by the rhetoric and practices of Empire. Laocratic movements are the political hope – because of the ambiguity of politics (i.e. politics can be seen in more than one way). Theology has a significant (but not totalizing) role in shifting the vision – so that there can be an utopian vision without it having to be fulfilled – 'let's be realists, demand the impossible' (Žižek) is the catch-phrase here.[44]

Empire constructs people in a particular way and depends on people's self-concept for its imperialistic achievements, although the three express it more technically, 'we refer to those conditions of subjectivity and of cultural self-conception that Empire generates in itself and in others, but that are simultaneously a result and a condition of its mode of establishing its politics and of exercising its economic dominance'.[45] We ought not to picture 'Empire' as comprising an emperor, his court, armies, treasury, fortified strongholds and systems of administrative and legal bureaucracy. Instead, we should conceive of empire 'as a way of exercising power through different legalities (and illegalities)'.[46] It is most certainly a system that favours elites and relies on them finding sufficiently overlapping interests. Securing outcomes to the elites' advantage comes through not only the possibilities that corporations can provide

---

44 Néstor Míguez *et al.*, *Beyond the Spirit of Empire: Theology and Politics in a New Key*, London: SCM Press, 2009, p. 109.

45 Míguez *et al.*, *Beyond*, p. 1.

46 Míguez *et al.*, *Beyond*, p. 3.

commercially, but through far less organizational systems. Crucial to empire is the limited capacity that national governments have to operate the levers and pulleys of control or regulatory schemes.[47]

Neoliberal economics represents an obvious manifestation of the imperial reach: only free competition in all the spheres of life can produce true liberty, and any interference will only reduce the possibilities for human expression.[48] We are encouraged to view one another not as neighbours, but primarily as competitors. All do not, of course, have equal competitive strength, access to resources, or options to choose from. Most of the world is rendered subaltern below those who benefit from economic advantage. What is crucial for any discussion of theological critique is the by now familiar notion that we (whether advantaged or subaltern) are shaped by Empire. We absorb its model of the human subject and so internalize that sense of self; scarcely aware, even if at all, of what is being done to us. As the three authors express it, '[t]he dominant symbolic structure is integrated into the expressions of those rendered subaltern within it, and they end up incorporating this symbolic into their self-images'.[49]

Such a picture is pretty bleak and, if we are not careful, falls under Petrella's criticism of gigantism, leaving us paralysed. However, coming to consciousness of imperial shaping is possible and occurs in actual and usually hard-pressed conditions. Such self-transcendence or awareness does not itself bring down Empire but in, what Jürgen Moltmann has argued to be the freedom *of God* in history: 'transformations of God',[50] 'anticipations'[51] or *'praesentia*

---

47 '[Empire's] formation is built on its capacity to bring together the interests of certain elites, beyond different institutional organizational possibilities and without decisive influence from national or ethnic limitations, and on its capacity to mobilize the strengths of a different order for those interests and to avoid the controls and balances that regulate the exercise of power' (Míguez *et al.*, *Beyond*, p. 3).

48 Míguez, *et al.*, *Beyond*, p. 14.

49 Míguez, *et al.*, *Beyond*, p. 19.

50 Moltmann, *Crucified God*, p. 321.

51 Moltmann, *Crucified God*, p. 273.

explosiva'.[52] This might otherwise be understood as chinks of light in the darkness that cannot overcome the light:

> We do not say, as some argue, that the power that will destroy the Empire is in the most humble, poor, meek, excluded, and marginalised. This would place tremendous responsibility on their shoulders, another burden. We are saying that, in its unwelcome presence, in its impossible disguise, in the deaths and crosses painted on the wall of shame, the spirit of Empire is revealed, and in the face of this spirit of death, from the reserve of antihegemonic feelings of the people, the spirit of life is expressed.[53]

In Western contexts – and remembering Petrella's point about the 'Third' world being also present in the 'First' – we encounter Empire most significantly in its form of consumerism. This is the dominant way in which the self is constructed – not simply our political and economic structures.[54] Who we think we are, our identity, our perceived scope for agency – what we can call our subjectivity – is shaped by the religion of the free market. Not just our jobs, but our subjectivity is made subservient to the needs of capital accumulation 'which has become an end in itself under the conditions of capitalism'.[55] Certainly, we are attached (to varying degrees) to our possessions, but more significantly 'the relations between things unconsciously shape the relations between human beings and thus human subjectivity at its deepest levels, including religion'.[56]

On the one hand, we are encouraged to imitate other people's desires (mimetic desire), so we have to obtain a new tablet computer not because we need it but because we perceive that others need it and, so mimetic desire goes, I too must 'need' it – so I want it. Integral to this idea of mimetic desire is the balancing of

---

52 Moltmann, *Crucified God*, p. 338.
53 Míguez *et al.*, *Beyond*, p. 22.
54 Míguez *et al.*, *Beyond*, p. 26.
55 Míguez *et al.*, *Beyond*, p. 35.
56 Míguez *et al.*, *Beyond*, p. 36.

society required in the face of escalating imitation that cannot be satisfied. There must be scapegoats, people sacrificed in terms of position, what they can acquire and, in the consequences of abject poverty and disease, their very lives. Within the neoliberal imperial economic – and cultural – system '[t]he sacrificed are those who appear less competent, who resist the laws of the market, and those who seek to regulate the market'.[57] Circulating within the system, reinforcing and attempting to control is a language of omnipotence practised by what we may recognize from the Allies' Iraq ventures as 'shock and awe'. Beyond that particular battlefield a critique of Empire seeks to unmask what it finds as a more widespread strategy of managing competing desires – to the advantage always of the elites:

> On the side of the perpetrators and others who benefit from this situation, there is a sense of power and control that is hard to achieve anywhere else in real life and resembles the sort of omnipotent power that borders on classical theist images of the divine. On the side of all those who are not in control, whether abducted and tortured or not, there is a sense of vulnerability and danger that resides in the symbolic order just as much as in reality.[58]

This forming of our subjectivity occurs in such a way that we are unaware of how things look from the underside.[59] We might have very clearly differentiated categories, and even pride ourselves in being able to recognize others' difference but, in the spirit of Empire, ours are idealized images (variously romanticized or demonized) of 'the poor', 'immigrants', 'welfare recipients' etc. The problem is that it is we, the advantaged, who are deciding what others are 'really like' for we, so we believe, understand them better than they understand themselves.[60]

---

57 Míguez *et al.*, *Beyond*, p. 40.
58 Míguez *et al.*, *Beyond*, p. 43.
59 Míguez *et al.*, *Beyond*, p. 46.
60 Míguez *et al.*, *Beyond*, p. 47.

Míguez, Rieger and Sung argue that the spirit of Empire relies on a mistaken understanding of transcendence through which the practice of sacrificing others is left unremarkable.[61] The trio drive the point home: 'Jung Mo Sung points out the magnitude of the conversion that is at stake here, when he considers Jesus' statement that God "desires mercy, not sacrifice" (Matt. 9.13) to be an epistemological revolution.'[62] What is needed, so they contend, is an alternative subjectivity – the laocratic movement that puts those sacrificed in neoliberal imperial economics *and culture* at the centre. This is more than a different political, democratic structure – although it does rely on democratic order.[63] It is a 'movement of force in which the useless and excluded are included as a question, critique, challenge and opposition to the current ruling system. To put it in terms of Jesus' parable, it is the unexpected presence of the beggars at the banquet (Luke 14.15–24).'[64] The laocratic movement, especially for a Christian perspective, is not necessarily violent, nor is it confined to the visible features of a revolution. Rather, the laocratic movement occurs also in 'breaches that allow the appearance of micropolitics as a space of resistance to Empire and of anticipation of other balances of power'.[65]

What is demanded, then, of Practical Theology?

We seem to have come a long way in articulating the critique of Petrella against US Liberation Theology and the three authors – Míguez, Rieger and Sung – on what is required of a truly liberative Christianity in the face of neoliberal imperialism. We have to see to what extent contemporary Practical Theology falls short – in order that we might advance an enhanced, dare I say *advanced*, version. Where is Practical Theology afflicted by monochromatism? What historical project is our field possibly forgetting? Where is

---

61 Míguez *et al.*, *Beyond*, p. 95.
62 Míguez *et al.*, *Beyond*, p. 150.
63 Míguez *et al.*, *Beyond*, p. 183.
64 Míguez *et al.*, *Beyond*, p. 176.
65 Míguez *et al.*, *Beyond*, p. 177.

there outrage – and what place does it have? Is Practical Theology sufficiently aware of the neoliberal shaping of subjectivity; the subjectivity of those who practise faith in our contexts? Where does Empire figure – and where ought it to figure – in practical theological reflection?

If Practical Theology is not to fall into the trap of being merely correlational (the liberal theological project), it will need to be radical in its goals, its critique, its self-critique and its methods. I am not suggesting that Practical Theology simply lashes itself to a flabby, dissipated and commodified Liberation Theology. The Practical Theology that we should seek to make more accessible to lay people – and in which experts in their own field can be mobilized – needs to be a sharper, much less bourgeois form of reflective practice.

But, this rather presumes that Practical Theology has been tested and found wanting. That has yet to be established. So, we turn to a case study: an evaluation of the recently published *Wiley-Blackwell Companion to Practical Theology* because it is, and will likely become, definitive for the discipline not only in North America but in the UK and much of Europe. It is not only bringing the story to us thus far, but in so doing is shaping the future of the discipline. That is not to say that it is the definitive word on our field, nor that we will all blindly implement its insights. Rather, it is one way in which I think I can evaluate Practical Theology as a discipline in the light of critiques that, we must remember, are directed in Petrella's case specifically at US liberation theologies, although Míguez, Rieger and Sung address theologies more generally.

7

Case Study: *The Wiley-Blackwell Companion to Practical Theology* – The Neoliberal, Imperialist Elephant in the Room?

The Wiley-Blackwell Companion to Practical Theology was published at the very end of 2011, and its 56 specially commissioned chapters (each of around 4,500 words) is the major attempt to 'organize, scrutinize, and advance' the discipline.[1] I am using it as a case study in the light of Petrella's criticisms of US Liberation Theology and of the more general challenge to theologies in the light of the spirit of Empire made by Míguez, Rieger and Sung. The *Companion* is already recognized variously as a 'showcase' (*Homiletic Journal*, 2012), an 'outstanding reference' (Mary Elizabeth Moore, Boston University) and as marking the coming of age of modern Practical Theology (Stephen Pattison, University of Birmingham, UK).[2]

In four major parts, the *Companion* looks, in order, at how Practical Theology is used in shaping faith among believers, how the discipline analyses practices (its methods), the relationship between Practical Theology and various sub-disciplines in educating people for ministry (largely the US seminary curriculum) and closes with a fourth part that reflects on the diverse ways in which, as a guild,

---

1 Bonnie J. Miller-McLemore, 'Introduction: The Contributions of Practical Theology', in Bonnie J. Miller-McLemore (ed.), *The Wiley-Blackwell Companion to Practical Theology*, Chichester: Wiley-Blackwell, 2012 (abbreviated to *Companion* from here on), p. 1.

2 Taken from Wiley website: http://eu.wiley.com/WileyCDA/WileyTitle/productCd-1444330829.html.

Practical Theology relates to issues and has developed differently in global regional and theological traditions. I am not reviewing each and every chapter, but it is worth noticing that it opens, to its credit, with an article on suffering; placing, as we would expect, the discussion of the discipline within the context of people's experience – and particularly that of pain and distress.[3]

The editor, Bonnie Miller-McLemore, is honest about the 'difficult-to-avoid imperialistic or colonialistic ordering of topics'.[4] I think she is correct in understanding her editorial task within a publishing regime that requires a book to be marketable:

> It is hard to challenge the prioritization of the Western academy and world when organizing a book that covers a discipline's Western development, written largely for a Western population most able to publish, buy and read books. To tell the story and to produce an intellectual product for market consumption almost unavoidably repeats the pathology of social and economic dominance and the repression of marginalized communities. The arrangement of chapters in the section on regions and religious traditions reflects this most explicitly.[5]

Miller-McLemore has to reflect the historical development of the discipline, so Continental Europe opens that part of the *Companion*. Nevertheless, 'Companions' and major reference works not only reflect a discipline, but also reproduce it, not least because we are dealing with imagined communities; the 'world' or 'guild' of Practical Theologians is a construction amenable to both reconfiguration but also consolidation. The Bible read page-by-page in its canonical ordering tells a somewhat different story than if it's read in the chronological sequence of the editing of its narratives. Simply not opening with the creation myths sets up a variant experience – with its own set of challenges. Without raising the *Companion* to the status of Scripture, the sequence of sections and, perhaps more significantly, within sections may well solidify the

---

3 Pamela Cooper-White, 'Suffering', in *Companion*, pp. 23–31.
4 Miller-McLemore, 'Introduction', p. 14.
5 Miller-McLemore, 'Introduction', p. 15.

'pathology' of dominance. At the same time, this might not be a wholly bad thing if, but only if, those treating it as a 'launching pad for further work' are able to overcome (or otherwise subvert) the power of publishing corporations.[6] Of course, postcolonialist works in Practical Theology will appear in greater numbers, but without diligent attention by our imagined community these will be but the marginalized, non-canonical equivalents of the Gospel of Thomas.

My approach to this case study is to first examine the chapters that, given their topic, are the most obvious places to look for a politically radical or liberation approach to questions of capitalism, neoliberalism and postcolonialist critiques. Then I will turn to consider chapters that, although positive in this regard, I think ought to have developed that line further. We'll then see those articles that, although still positive about a critique of capitalism and further postcolonial concerns, give these only minor attention. Finally, we will examine the topics where the omission of a liberation, globalization, postcolonial critique is particularly worrying. First, we can usefully give a roll call of those contributions that hit the spot.

Hitting the spot

Opening with her account of commencing a two-year-long US Peace Corps assignment in the Amazon region, Melinda McGarrah Sharp is clear about the ambiguities of intercultural encounter when one party is in such a position of economic advantage.[7] She is spot-on in identifying a similar ambiguity in the tension between self-reflection and learning with others in intercultural and asymmetrical encounters. Sharp hits on what Petrella has framed as amnesia – the actual conditions of people are forgotten:

> While the turn to internal critique is necessary, it can also implode so completely as to turn me toward myself and my struggles thereby losing the crucial connection to the intercultural reality

---

6 Miller-McLemore, 'Introduction', p. 15.

7 Melinda McGarrah Sharp, 'Globalization, Colonialism, and Post-colonialism', in *Companion*, p. 422.

that led to this knowledge. This feeds the temptation to continue to mask injustice both internally and in relationships with other people and institutions.[8]

Sharp also picks up on the necessity for Practical Theology to challenge its traditional conversation partner – psychology – with respect to the latter's power to name what is normal. Postcolonial psychologies, she argues, offer unmasking of, for example, intra-psychic conflict that is related to historical colonialism. The emphasis in Practical Theology upon embodiment also throws up complexities and assumptions around relating that carry colonizer–colonized dynamics. Although Sharp is able to find some practical theological work that highlights the globalization and colonial dimensions of intercultural encounter, she concludes that 'Practical Theology as a discipline has not grappled adequately with postcolonial theories and realities.'[9]

Joyce Ann Mercer asks, 'Why Practical Theology is afraid of economics and late to class' in her chapter 'Economics, Class, and Classism'.[10] Mercer pushes her sight beyond North America and gives due credit to Elaine Graham's work on social justice in the UK, alongside that of Pamela Couture (formerly in the USA, now in Canada). Mercer finds a turn towards economics in Practical Theology and brings our attention to works that recognize how class intersects with other identity frames such as race and gender. This crops up too for Practical Theologians from marginalized communities. Mercer brings our attention to Latina Nanko-Fernandez's observation that in order to be taken seriously, they need to navigate the hierarchies of theological disciplines. As a result, race, class and gender advantages demand that Practical Theologians position themselves in systematic theology or ethics; another factor, I would add, in the complexities of the imagined community that is Practical Theology.

---

8 Sharp, 'Globalization', p. 425.
9 Sharp, 'Globalization', p. 423.
10 Joyce Ann Mercer, 'Economics, Class, and Classism', in *Companion*, p. 433.

What most strikes me from Mercer's contribution to the *Companion* is her claim that one of the barriers to Practical Theology engaging in questions of classism in relation to economic disparities and inequalities is 'due in part to the national myth of America as a classless society. How can classism be confronted when there are no class differences?'[11]

There are a number of other places in the *Companion* where we would expect to find – and do indeed find – clear articulations of a liberation agenda and critique of neoliberalism. Pamela Couture's discussion on social policy describes, among others, her own work – including contributions to religious peace-making in the Democratic Republic of the Congo.[12] Nancy Ramsay traces the history of Liberation Theology as it relates specifically to Practical Theology.[13] Latina Elizabeth Conde-Frazier opens these aspects up in her piece on participatory action research, where social justice is to the fore in people educating themselves and engaging in consciousness raising. For me, the clearest statement is Miguel A. De La Torre's liberationist ethics – which we will consider in a little more depth in the next chapter. When we think of all the ethicists – many who identify themselves at least to some extent with Practical Theology – it is highly significant that the writer of this piece is one who is challenging the abstract, universalizing Western tradition.[14] The protest, affirmation and new creation themes of feminism, discussed by Elaine Graham, are, as we would expect, closely intertwined with, and generated from, liberationist standpoints and acutely conscious in the return to dealing with lived experience; how capitalism intersects with gender.[15] The regional account of the development of Practical Theology in Brazil is, unsurprisingly, woven around themes of economics, the World Social Forums, ecology and urban life for marginalized and disadvantaged people.[16]

---

11 Mercer, 'Economics', p. 434.

12 Pamela D. Couture, 'Social Policy', in *Companion*, pp. 153–62.

13 Nancy J. Ramsay, 'Emancipatory Theory and Method', in *Companion*, pp. 183–92.

14 Miguel A. De La Torre, 'Ethics', in *Companion*, pp. 337–46.

15 Elaine Graham, 'Feminist Theory', in *Companion*, pp. 193–203.

16 Valburga Schmiedt Streck, 'Brazil', in *Companion*, pp. 525–33.

It is worth mentioning here the strong articulation of postcolonial developments in African theologies that is offered in the chapter on West Africa.[17] However, I struggled to see how practical theological methods were being deployed and how these relate to African theologies. This, and the chapters on Brazil and South Korea, do pose questions for Practical Theology in a context of church *growth* rather than decline, especially where it is Evangelicalism (or Pentecostalism) that is the dominant tradition in those regions.[18]

A little off the target – but not by much

When discussing consumption, it is good to see recognition of the part played by the USA in global capitalism.[19] Katherine Turpin is well aware that it is indeed difficult for many Christians to question what is an organizing structure of everyday life for to do so 'would be tantamount to questioning deeply held common beliefs about the nature of the world and our purposes within it'.[20] She also gives us a small pointer towards questioning the ways in which Christian faith is part of, not apart from, a consumerist mind set that 'tap[s] into acquisitive desire to market Christian trinkets, books, personal decor and clothing'.[21] While Turpin is right to direct our attention to organizations that encourage alternative, simpler ways of living, her perspective is, to my mind, still too anchored to the predilections of middle-class (American) Christians. I know that Turpin, like the other authors, has to address the audience who can afford to buy this text or avail themselves of access to an educational institution that does so. Nevertheless, it is all well and good to reflect on consumption from the standpoint of the consumer, but a Practical

---

17 Daisy N. Nwachuku, 'West Africa', in *Companion*, pp. 515–24.
18 Meerha Hahn, 'South Korea', in *Companion*, pp. 534–43. While the *Companion* has chapters on both Evangelicalism and Pentecostalism, the field is at an early stage of incorporation and would need to break from its liberal, and perhaps also liberation, roots to do so more extensively.
19 Katherine Turpin, 'Consuming', in *Companion*, pp. 70–9.
20 Turpin, 'Consuming', p. 73.
21 Turpin, 'Consuming', p. 76.

Theology discussion would look quite different if those unable to afford to participate, those whom Zygmunt Bauman finds to be treated as 'flawed consumers', are centre-stage.[22] (As an aside, a chapter on religious leadership would have been an ideal place to open out questions around the pastor as a conveyor of capitalist, commodified Christianity.)[23]

We see a similar problem arising in Lee Butler Jr's chapter on psychological theory. His attention to liberationist approaches connect psychology to issues of social justice.[24] I do wonder, however, about the economics of psychological care – particularly, but not only, that offered within the sphere of Christian ministries. What does Practical Theology have to say about the purchase of counselling care and the commodification of healthcare more widely? Perhaps once again it is the US context that obscures what is more readily obvious to a reader in a Scottish National Health Service – publicly funded and free at the point of need.[25]

Before continuing, I want to reiterate my earlier point that the *Companion* has to deal with Practical Theology as it currently is. I cannot expect authors, within the constraints of 4,500 words, to give comprehensive coverage – even though therein lies the danger of readers choosing to take this as confirmation of their own limited horizons. In that vein, while Heather Walton's discussion of the importance of the work of Rebecca Chopp (whose concerns, as we have seen, chime very much with a challenge to the economics of Empire), the voice of poetics in Practical Theology still emerges as a very Western one.[26] Perhaps the small corpus of womanist works in Practical Theology that Evelyn Parker identifies can prove a broader stimulus to postcolonial perspectives; although it might fall foul of Petrella's charge of monochromatism.[27]

---

22 Zygmunt Bauman, *Work, Consumerism and the New Poor*, Buckingham: Open University Press, 1990.

23 Michael Jinkins, 'Religious Leadership', in *Companion*, pp. 308–17.

24 Lee H. Butler Jr, 'Psychological Theory', in *Companion*, p. 110.

25 I think my Scottish context is crucial here given the moves in England towards a less publicly funded service.

26 Heather Walton, 'Poetics', in *Companion*, pp. 173–82.

27 Evelyn L. Parker, 'Womanist Theory', in *Companion*, pp. 204–13.

Signs of further hope

I now turn to a category of chapters where it is good to find some, occasionally surprising, recognition of capitalism and the importance of challenge to Empire. John Swinton's piece on disability is particularly strong on liberation, and he makes the important point that systems of economic exchange (capitalism) need redefining rather than allowing those systems of exchange to define the able over against the dis-abled person.[28] Likewise, Claire Wolfteich is careful to connect spirituality to justice – a linkage, I would add, that can by no means be taken for granted among those whose relationship with themselves, others and God is profoundly moulded by Empire.[29] The commendation that Sally Brown makes of Pieterse's work on poverty in South Africa and the implications of preaching there is a welcome one in the context of a discussion of hermeneutical theory.[30] Similarly, Ruard Ganzevoort recognizes the importance of subaltern voices in his chapter on narrative approaches.[31] His conclusion that narrative theory can become 'too cerebral, verbal, and cognitive' is equally welcome, reflecting his commitment to embodiment and the full range of human expression that is otherwise readily bracketed out by Western rationalist privilege.[32]

As we might expect, an enlightened model of religious education in the *Companion* makes a key element of the argument the need to locate and attend to questions lurking in the margins – rather than a banking, didactic emphasis in learning.[33] So too, although more surprisingly to me given the rather different meaning of 'biblical theology' to a British reader, is the highlighting of a black theological lens in reading the Bible alongside other lenses.[34] The

---

28 John Swinton, 'Disability, Ableism, and Disablism', in *Companion*, p. 447.

29 Claire E. Wolfteich, 'Spirituality', in *Companion*, p. 331.

30 Sally A. Brown, 'Hermeneutical Theory', in *Companion*, p. 120.

31 R. Ruard Ganzevoort, 'Narrative Approaches', in *Companion*, p. 214.

32 Ganzevoort, 'Narrative Approaches', p. 222.

33 Carol Lakey Hess, 'Religious Education', in *Companion*, pp. 299–307.

34 Michael Joseph Brown, 'Biblical Theology', in *Companion*, pp. 112–22.

contemporary deploying of methods of what we in the UK prefer to call 'church history' struck me as perhaps more innovative than it ought when a discussion of the relationship between historical and Practical Theology is illustrated by a student fieldtrip to Guatemala.[35]

Now we come to those chapters where I think we ought to expect to see more overt consideration given – even if only limited – to some of the cluster of critiques of neoliberalism and Empire; in fact, to postcolonial and liberationist concerns in general.

Missing the mark

Let me start with absolving the chapter on race and racism. Dale Andrews can only deal with the situation as it is – and Practical Theology (in the USA) is part of church traditions and practices that are conflicted about racism and ambiguous in their responses.[36] It is disappointing that so few connections are possible with Practical Theology – although a UK picture could be a little different.[37] The problem of the US-centrism haunting this text reaches its zenith in the regional discussion of the USA.[38] Rick Osmer's account of the historical development of Practical Theology is excellent, but where is the contemporary defining aspect of US identity: the nexus of war, military industries, security and nationalism? Voices critical of US policy and cultural tropes in this cluster of themes may not be from those self-identifying as Practical Theologians. That in itself is worthy of critical reflection, but the issues are missing from the *Companion* as a whole.[39] Reading the 600 pages you would never know that Practical Theology is a discipline performed in a world

35 James M. Brandt, 'Historical Theology', in *Companion*, pp. 367–76.

36 Dale P. Andrews, 'West Africa', in *Companion*, p. 407.

37 This point is made, in regards to the *Companion*'s chapter by Kathleen Greider on religious pluralism, see below (but it is equally relevant to race relations), by one of the Anglia Ruskin Group in Various: 'Review: The Wiley-Blackwell Companion to Practical Theology', *Practical Theology* 7.1 (2014), p. 70.

38 Richard R. Osmer, 'The United States', in *Companion*, pp. 495–504.

39 The only reference to US military power that I could find in the *Companion* was Couture, 'Social Policy', p. 159.

with multiple wars and a vast military complex of US superiority. Iraq and Afghanistan are airbrushed out of the bigger picture of practical theological reflection.

There may have been issues around marketing a major book to a US audience that is not ready to hear a practical theological critique of core dimensions of their national identity. Nevertheless, the impression that is left is detrimental to the discipline and one that makes Petrella's, Míguez, Rieger and Sung's criticisms of theology even more relevant.

There is something of a blind spot here, because in the chapter on the Protestant evangelical context for Practical Theology there is but a small mention of the Religious Right – but it is historical.[40] The *Companion* seems to shy away from demonstrating the importance of practical theological critique of such movements. Somehow the liberal and liberationist antennae fail US Practical Theologians in this publication.

If we move to other contributions, the discussion of religious pluralism is another that would have benefited from a wider (perhaps British) perspective.[41] It did strike me that Kathleen Greider's piece would have also benefited from the voice of those at the sharp-end of interreligious violence.

The chapter on worship missed an opportunity to highlight the importance of reflecting on this dimension of Christian practice quite politically – not only with reference to capitalism, but also nationalism and war.[42] When so many US Christians worship in churches that are unashamedly American, it is incumbent upon Practical Theology to put this under scrutiny. A similar criticism can be made of the article on integration in theological education. It is absolutely right to see that questions of the self are to be explored in relation to vocation and 'the complex challenges of postmodern society'.[43] However, the shaping of subjectivity by

---

40 Charles J. Scalise, 'Protestant Evangelicalism', in *Companion*, p. 580.

41 Kathleen J. Greider, 'Religious Pluralism and Christian-Centrism', in *Companion*, pp. 452–62.

42 Don E. Saliers, 'Worship', in *Companion*, pp. 289–98.

43 Kathleen A. Cahalan, 'Integration in Theological Education', in *Companion*, p. 388.

the Empire through neoliberal economic values and practices does not feature in Cahalan's analysis. Christian Scharen's discussion of blessing almost reads like a defence of owning a second (holiday) home.[44] Granted, he is partly apologetic and makes a stab at arguing that a holiday home contributes to the local economy; however, more than a nod towards those who 'die daily of the simple lack of food, clean water, and basic medicine' is required.[45] What does 'blessing' mean from within that experience? Petrella's criticisms are highly germane.

The chapter on loving seems to me a very 'middle American' presentation. I am willing to concede that this stereotyping might be somewhat harsh, but I come back to the glaring absence of war that pervades this volume. What does Practical Theology have to say about loving, when you experience poverty and seemingly endemic violence – not necessarily on the battlefields of Iraq, but in the urban centres (and some rural communities) of the USA? The discussion of eating has tiny hints of the hungry, but not in terms of systemic poverty and there is no voice of the hungry – again voices from within the USA could tell a very different story; Bass would not have to go too far afield.[46]

The point I have made about the economics of counselling care can be made too of the chapter on healing. Susan Dunlop offers two good contextual studies – one a Pentecostal, the other a liberal Protestant – but says nothing about healthcare economics in the USA and the relationship between health and poverty.[47] The pattern of missing the experience of the marginalized and systematically disadvantaged emerges also in Pamela Cooper-White's chapter that opens the contributions. She gives a nod towards a liberationist perspective, but firmly locates the relevance of Practical Theology to suffering in the context of therapy with just a nod towards social justice elements.[48]

---

44 Christian Scharen, 'Blessing', in *Companion*, p. 87.
45 Scharen, 'Blessing', p. 87.
46 Dorothy C. Bass, 'Eating', in *Companion*, pp. 51–60. This point is made by the Anglia Ruskin review group in Various, 'Review', p. 64.
47 Susan J. Dunlop, 'Healing', in *Companion*, pp. 32–41.
48 Cooper-White, 'Suffering', pp. 28, 29, 30.

Overall assessment

There is much that is excellent about this *Companion*, in its scope and level of analysis. It is indeed a landmark piece of work that should have a significant place in the advancing of our discipline. I have confined my assessment to a narrow but – as I have argued from Petrella and the others – vital perspective. I am not going to attempt to rate the *Companion* on an imaginary scale of 'imperialist and neoliberal critique'. However, as a case study I think it confirms the saliency of such a challenge to the way in which Practical Theology is framed. At the very least, silence over the neoliberal and imperialist elephant in the room – war and nationalism – has to give us considerable cause for concern.

8

Radicalizing Practical Theology

In a changing world a major question for us here is how Practical Theology can be, to use the phrase beloved of politicians taking a snipe at an inconvenient institution, 'fit for purpose'. Updating is a ubiquitous concept in our experience of using computers. Fixes and enhancements are delivered sometimes with the rapidity that raises questions about the readiness of an application for public release in the first place. 'Oh, sorry, that last service we did to your car immobilized the brakes. But don't worry, just bring it back when you can and we'll install a fix.' Perish the thought that my garage ran its workflow like some app developers. Perhaps Practical Theology could benefit from an update – but I'm not convinced that really captures the realignment I have in mind. 'Unsettling Practical Theology' has the benefit of two meanings: the discipline requires unsettling, and it is a way of doing theology that unsettles people. However, I think we need a stronger word because of the shaping power of ideas and actions that weigh so heavily in favour of the already-privileged. I did, momentarily, toy with heading this chapter 'Extremist Practical Theology', but that was too contentious.

'Fanatical Practical Theology' has a certain *je ne sais quoi* about it – as long as we Practical Theologians reserve to ourselves its use. I would be a tad unhappy for others to deploy it as a term of abuse. 'Militant Practical Theology' has a lot going for it, and I quite like the idea of 'Rebel Practical Theology' (if it weren't for sci-fi movies having put too many images of 'rebel alliance' in my mind). For reasons that will become clear later, 'reforming' and 'revolutionary' don't quite position Practical Theology in the way I would care to. 'Radicalizing' seems to fit the bill, although I'm well aware that radicalization is steeped in negative associations and will come to that later.

The right kind of reflexivity

'Reconstructing Practical Theology' is quite close to the tone I want to set, and I share many concerns with John Reader who has helpfully articulated his vision of how Practical Theology needs to take cognizance of globalization. He demonstrates how we need to acknowledge that the world in which we practise critical discipleship is not the world of a few decades ago. We have to deal with boundaries between nations, cultures and religions that are blurred but at the same time are defended, often vociferously or violently.[1] The way we conceive of space is, within globalization, one that is not so much geographical as it is experiential. In other words, our house is still concrete enough, but our relationships with people (and thus to a large extent with ourselves) are not confined to a geographical area or two but distributed across the world in different time zones. In many ways, like our finances (it's probably not helpful to think here of 'money' with its connotations of paper or even gold that we could touch), our relationships are flowing in and out of cyberspace. Not that such flows are merely ephemeral or inconsequential. It is decisions made across – and often without regard for – national boundaries that materially affect our lives.

Reader also identifies our ambivalent feeling of being simultaneously enclosed by the global capitalist system (here we are in the language of Empire again) yet still aware of the thresholds or margins where resistance is not futile.[2] The people, we, who are shaped among blurred boundaries, enclosed yet aware of thresholds, are thrown back on our own resources to make something of ourselves. Within globalization the familiar, longstanding structures are being undermined so that these no longer offer us the ready-made

---

1 John Reader, *Reconstructing Practical Theology: The Impact of Globalization*, Aldershot: Ashgate, 2008, pp. 9f.

2 Reader, *Reconstructing*, p. 14. The hint at the Borg is, I confess, mine and not Reader's.

frameworks in which, and through which, our predecessors might once have found and made their individuality. In one sense we have much more choice than previous generations, but the extent of choice can be both exhilarating and paralysing. Reader realizes that this destabilizing experience – in sociological terms, 'reflexive modernization' – has serious implications for Practical Theology.

He makes us alert to the quite different roots and assumptions behind the practice of reflexivity or reflection that Practical Theology has promoted. Its model comes from psychotherapy and educational development in which being reflective means 'a self-conscious pursuit of greater self-awareness that leads to heightened understanding and control over one's life'.[3] Instead, Reader recognizes the sociological perspective on reflexivity that focuses on global processes 'that undermine the previous structures of social and personal life' meaning that, even if the necessary resources are taken away, diminished or inaccessible, we still have to construct our own life.[4]

Reader sets out the aspects he believes Practical Theology needs to address in the light of globalization – not being left using outdated, 'zombie categories'.[5] Churches cannot, he argues, work with ideas and practices of space (in the sense of geographical locality), when people have very different senses of place. This means handling people's greater mobility – not just in terms of transport or movement, but with regard to the attachments that are formed. Project Self – my task of lifelong construction of who I am – is significantly impacted by consumer cultures. Reader has a good stab at defining this ambition as 'project identity … the capacity of human subjects to envision different and alternative futures'.[6] While this affects the sorts of pastoral care that a local church might seek to

---

3 Reader, *Reconstructing*, p. 16.

4 Reader, *Reconstructing*, p. 16.

5 Reader, following Ulrich Beck, explains: 'Zombie categories are "the living dead", the tried and familiar frameworks of interpretation that have served us well for many years and continue to haunt our thoughts and analyses, even though they are embedded in a world that is passing away before our eyes' (Reader, *Reconstructing*, p. 1).

6 Reader, *Reconstructing*, p. 46.

offer, Project Self points, as Reader rightly acknowledges, towards a much more political understanding of pastoral care. We are back here to attending to the ways in which we are being shaped – not only through personal relationships, but by cultural, social and political structures that themselves carry and reinforce behaviour.

Reader selects the Eucharist as the focus of his discussion of Christian engagement with globalization in the form of worship and spirituality. Although he is sympathetic to some of the possibilities held out by William Cavanaugh's proposal that we make as much use as we can of the Eucharist as 'a story which performs spatial operations on places',[7] Reader is correct to challenge the idea that the Church can (or ought to) be 'the privileged locus for resistance'.[8] His suggestion that it might be 'networks and/or individuals who stand more of a chance of creating convincing alternatives' is not too far from Petrella's figures who are 'undercover' Liberation Theologians within corporations or organizations.[9] Reader concludes that the (Western, capitalist) world in which Practical Theology operates, a world in which the authority of tradition is being dismantled, requires 'reflexive spirituality'. This is 'the path of a greater articulation and defence of [the Christian tradition's] beliefs and the exercise of reflexivity, or a critical questioning self-awareness by its individual adherents'.[10] Reader goes on to give some shape to reflexive spirituality in relation to globalization of families, children, work and the new economy.

While I endorse Reader's deeply insightful reconstruction of Practical Theology, I think a still more radical dimension is required. This is for two main reasons, the intransigence of the rational subject of modernity and the tendency for Christians to privilege service over justice.

---

7 Reader, *Reconstructing*, p. 57.

8 Reader, *Reconstructing*, p. 57.

9 Reader, *Reconstructing*, p. 57. This is not to say that Reader would necessarily support Petrella's theology of what is the potential sacramental possibilities of the social sciences nor the decoupling of 'theology' from 'Liberation Theology'.

10 Reader, *Reconstructing*, p. 72.

'I shall not be moved'

Dutch Practical Theologian Riet Bons-Storm took issue with the 1997 conference theme of the International Academy of Practical Theology: 'Globalization and Difference: Conflict, Reconciliation and Transformation'.[11] Bons-Storm saw that the title disguised an assumption that the only difficult element in the triad was 'conflict'. 'Globalization' and 'contextualization' had become, so she argued, so familiar that they had lost their truly disturbing dimensions: 'We face the struggle between our need for a certain foundation-alism that gives us security, but tends to impose our foundations on others, on the one hand, and a frightening relativism, that gives room to the others, on the other.'[12] She was pointing out the full implications of viewing all opinions as 'constructions of local truth conceptions'.[13] Now here is not the place to defend or support her thorough-going contextualizing of theology.[14] Instead, it is Bons-Storm's observation of what an attenuated appreciation of contextualization resorts to that is important. She identifies a retreat into the idea of 'One Knowable Truth' as the foundationalism that gives security. From this standpoint – crucially posited as univer-sal (although contextual) – other people are benchmarked. Such others (approached as non-males, non-whites, non-heterosexuals, non-middle-classes) 'are deep down perceived as not so identifiable with the rational subject of modernity'.[15] Bons-Storm's alternative configuration is to view our differences as a virtue, but that a path

---

11 Riet Bons-Storm, 'Thinking and Living Diversities in Practical The-ology', in Paul H. Ballard and Pamela D. Couture (eds), *Globalization and Difference: Practical Theology in a World Context*, Fairwater, Cardiff: Cardiff Academic Press, 1999, pp. 123–27.

12 Bons-Storm, 'Thinking', p. 123.

13 Bons-Storm, 'Thinking', p. 123.

14 We will see the further importance of resisting universalizing approaches when we consider Miguel A. De La Torre on liberative ethics later.

15 Bons-Storm, 'Thinking', p. 123. She lists 'persons from out of Europe and North America, all non-university-educated persons and all women', but I think the point is more clearly made if we use the dominant category and, as it does, render others as not-that.

from the conflict of modernity to the possibilities of reconciliation will make for a difficult journey.[16]

Modernity (symbolic here of the domination of the already-advantaged, threatened by difference) is alive and kicking – not least within the Empire that relies for its power on globalized, decentralized, flows of finance and neoliberal influence. In this respect, a zombie category serves us well by *not* being dead. It highlights the enduring disadvantage that globalization fosters at the very same time as globalization lures with enticements of consumer prosperity.

The contribution by Herbert Anderson to the same volume of conference papers highlights beautifully the implications for Practical Theology – albeit unintentionally. Anderson articulated a *habitus* or 'disposition of the soul' that he believed would address globalization.[17] Engaging with the other would require wonder, hospitality, recognition and reconciliation. Despite Anderson's obvious sincere compassion, the 'we' referred to in his piece is a 'we' who, if not wholly innocent, is not really too guilty of causing the suffering of the others. What comes through is a *habitus* from advantage – how else would practices of repentance be absent from Anderson's scheme? Granted, he appreciates that forgetting wrongdoing cannot be a feature of the process in a hasty move towards reconciliation. However, the vast imbalances within the spectrum of globalization's advantaged and disadvantaged fail to be treated sufficiently seriously. He tells us that in reconciliation 'all the voices are heard, every position has an equal hearing', but this is the language of the independent counsellor or mediator – a perspective within Practical Theology that is perhaps so prevalent as to obscure its limitations and influence upon the way proposals are framed.[18]

---

16 Bons-Storm, 'Thinking', p. 127.

17 Herbert Anderson, 'Seeing the Other Whole: A Habitus for Globalization', in Paul H. Ballard and Pamela D. Couture (eds), *Globalization and Difference: Practical Theology in a World Context*, Fairwater, Cardiff: Cardiff Academic Press, 1999, p. 6.

18 Anderson, 'Seeing', p. 15.

'Brother, sister, let me serve you … but let's not mention justice'

Coming more up to the present, Susanne Johnson identifies a similar problem in distancing from the other while purporting to pay attention to difference. Johnson tackles the implications behind Christian churches and organizations delivering social or welfare services to their community in the USA – in some cases with state or federal funding. (Her points could be equally germane to the British context of Third Sector participation by faith-based organizations.) Johnson examines how service-delivery is a mutation of what Christians have traditionally understood as servanthood. She takes Craig Dykstra's defence of service-delivery to task for 'to a great extent it mirrors mainline, middle-class piety which itself is riddled with unseen, unacknowledged class interests, ideologies, and distorted views of power and authority'.[19] 'His methodology', argues Johnson, *'privileges service over justice'*.[20] Dykstra adopts the common Christian argument of renouncing power in favour of servanthood. What this actually does, according to Johnson, is obscure the ways in which power is being retained: 'By renouncing power (or pretending to), we have exercised the greatest power of all: the power to conceal, the power to define, the power not to question the status quo, the power to determine the agenda.'[21] Dykstra and typical Christian responses in this mode pay close attention to relationships between people, but not to systemic advantages for the privileged 'servants':

Dykstra directs attention to *interpersonal* and *intersubjective* relationships – diverting attention away from how systems and ideologies (such as white privilege and class bias) often play a

---

19 Susanne Johnson, 'Remembering the Poor: Transforming Christian Practice', in Dana R. Wright and John D. Kuentzel (eds), *Redemptive Transformation in Practical Theology: Essays in Honor of James E. Loder Jr.*, Grand Rapids, MI, and Cambridge, UK: William B. Eerdmans, 2004, p. 200. Johnson is discussing Craig Dykstra, *Vision and Character: A Christian Educator's Alternative to Kohlberg*, New York: Paulist Press, 1981.
20 Johnson, 'Remembering', p. 201.
21 Johnson, 'Remembering', p. 213.

profound role in shaping and structuring, allowing and disallow-
ing, certain relationships in the first place.[22]

While it is problematic to talk of a centre and margins within the
categories of globalization either as geographical or dichotomous
terms, I think we still need to foreground this aspect if we are to
advance Practical Theology. If the global financial crisis has shown
us anything, it is that there is a qualitative as well as quantitative
difference between being caught up in such a storm on an ocean
liner or on a rubber dinghy. The experience is unpleasant for both
categories of travellers, but throwing up the evening's *foie gras* into
the toilet bowl in a first class cabin ought not to be compared with
wondering where the next sip of fresh water might come from in an
uncovered dinghy.

Admittedly, the various national economic recessions have had
significant implications for some middle-class people who have lost
management salaries and been faced with continuing to service
large mortgages and the multiple fees associated with privileged
lifestyle choices. The recession has played into the hands of those
neoliberal politicians for whom the welfare state has to be, ideo-
logically, as thin as possible under any economic circumstances.
Political interventions in the UK have sought to contract disability welfare allowances – through, widely perceived to be draconian
and ill-judged, assessments of people by private companies picking
up formerly state, but now outsourced, responsibilities. Controversial reductions in housing benefit have been imposed where an
additional bedroom is deemed, bureaucratically, to be surplus to
minimum requirements. This affects the lives of families for whom
a spare bedroom in Granny's house is vital to hers being their communal base. To lose 14 per cent from your housing benefit can
be highly significant to an already-low household budget in which
there is no disposable income. Long-term rhetoric in the Right-
wing press has, if not actually inculcating, surely contributed to
the public perception that £24 in every £100 spent from the welfare budget in the UK is fraudulently claimed; when the actual

---

22 Johnson, 'Remembering', p. 203.

figure is a mere 70 pence.[23] The climate of disparaging the materially disadvantaged members of our communities is no respecter of
the niceties of globalization's blurred boundaries and distributed
systems. In the competition for limited resources the power to
name and claim advantage come to the surface in the dichotomies
that have never really gone away.

Zombie categories can be looked at, as Reader quite correctly
does, as outdated, dead ways of framing our response to globalization. Yet, the significant feature of zombies is that they are the
animated or walking-dead. They are not redundant, but still moving
around. Even in this undead–unliving state zombie categories hold
some promise as reminders of who benefits and, conversely, who
does not benefit. Practical Theology needs to be exceedingly careful that it engages with globalization as a modern phenomenon and
not just a postmodern one. This is not to deny that economic marginalization is also distributed in the countries of greatest economic
prosperity. Poverty coexists alongside wealth in Florida, New York,
London or Amsterdam; as it does (although with the proportions
of people inverted) in Mumbai, Hong Kong or Buenos Aires. Practical Theology needs to be radical and radicalized if it is to take the
globalized conditions of people's lives seriously.

Reclaimed radicalization

It might seem at best unwise and at worst inflammatory to couch
Practical Theology and critical discipleship in terms of radicalization. As part of a constellation of responses to terrorist threats,
states are often making vigorous, if not always successful, efforts
to prevent people being radicalized. The general association
is between radicalization and extremist forms of Islamic faith. I
should not have to say so, but I will in order to avoid any doubt:
the radicalization of Practical Theology that I advance is non-violent. In
order to reclaim radicalism and the positive value of radicalization I

---

23 Ipsos MORI, *Perils of Perception* (London: Royal Statistical Society,
King's College London and Ipsos MORI, 2013). The mean figure of £24
was given by respondents to the survey.

want to set both in a theological context – specifically in relation to Christ. The discussion that Dietrich Bonhoeffer offers in his *Ethics* – granted in the quite different political, social and theological context of Nazi Germany – can help us advance an appropriately radical Practical Theology in our time.

In Christ there is neither radical nor compromiser

In order to appreciate Bonhoeffer's argument about radicalism and compromise we need first to set it, as he does, within the context of his particular use of two terms: the ultimate and the penultimate. The ultimate is his way of expressing the 'justification of the sinner by grace alone'; as God's Last Word.[24] The penultimate is Bonhoeffer's way of articulating the biblical assertion that justification is 'not only by grace alone, but also by faith alone'.[25] The life of grace-enabled faith is lived in the moments of everyday life and, crucially, it will be through actual living that someone will have been brought by God's grace to the encounter of justification or conversion. So, the penultimate is neither only the period before justification, nor solely the period of working out that salvation in a life of faithful actions. The penultimate is both but, crucially, it is only that which comes before the last – everyday life is important but 'the ultimate entirely annuls and invalidates it' as a means to justification.[26]

The problem that Bonhoeffer wants to explore is how a Christian is to relate the ultimate and the penultimate. He offers a concrete example – and for many this is a familiar one – of the challenges this can throw up. We are with someone who has been recently bereaved, and we find ourselves responding with silent solidarity; words are inadequate, and particularly words of Christian faith in the resurrection and God's comfort seem quite out of place at this point. We choose the solidarity of silence; the solidarity of the

---

24 Dietrich Bonhoeffer, *Ethics*, ed. Eberhard Bethge, London: SCM Press, 1955, p. 79.

25 Bonhoeffer, *Ethics*, p. 80.

26 Bonhoeffer, *Ethics*, p. 83.

penultimate. Do we thus betray the ultimate – God's Last Word of grace? The answer might seem obvious to we who are familiar with the grief process and even the most rudimentary of pastoral skills. Nevertheless, Bonhoeffer is not satisfied with offering us a pragmatic, even compassionate, answer.

Bonhoeffer identifies two extreme solutions in how people relate the ultimate to the penultimate. One is the radical solution in which Christ, as indeed God's Last Word, the Word of Judgement, is to drive our everyday life and decisions such as that when faced with a grieving friend. It is the stance that Bonhoeffer captures as, '[no] matter if the whole order of the world breaks down under the impact of the word of Christ, there must be no holding back'.[27] The opposite solution is the compromise. The world of everyday life is given priority and the ultimate – God's Last Word – is temporarily bracketed out. It is, so this solution goes, much more important to deal with people as they actually are – in this, the penultimate. Whereas the radical's is a solution of 'icy hardness', the compromiser's is unremitting mercy.[28]

The problem as Bonhoeffer sees it is that both those extremes (one the mirror image of the other) mistakenly set the penultimate and ultimate as mutually exclusive. Instead, Bonhoeffer turns our attention to Christ who is neither radical (in this sense) nor a compromiser (in this sense). Bonhoeffer is correct to observe that to argue over which is the more passionate or earnest approach is a mistake; but not for the reason we might immediately think. It is not a competition, because neither is earnest when, rather than human sincerity, eagerness or compassion, Christ is the sole example of what earnestness means. To let the competitive framework prevail is to reduce Christianity to a social system of beliefs, rather like a political or philosophical manifesto about which questions of who is more earnest than others is a perfectly reasonable question to ask. Rather:

> what is earnest and serious is not some kind of Christianity, but it is Jesus Christ Himself. And in Jesus Christ there is neither

---

27 Bonhoeffer, *Ethics*, p. 86.
28 Bonhoeffer, *Ethics*, p. 86.

radicalism nor compromise, but there is the reality of God and men. There is no Christianity in itself, for this would destroy the world; there is no man in himself, for he would exclude God. Both of these are merely ideas; only the God-Man Jesus Christ is real, and only through Him will the world be preserved until it is ripe for its end.[29]

The radical is, argues Bonhoeffer, unable to see that Christ gifts her the possibility of being reconciled to the world that she so vehemently hates in her radicalism. The compromiser, on the other hand, fails to appreciate the gift of freedom from the world because of her adaptability and dependence on worldly wise methods.

Bonhoeffer believes that the difficulty we have in relating the ultimate to the penultimate is because we 'tear ... apart' the incarnation, crucifixion and resurrection of Christ into separate, disconnected doctrines.[30] In more concrete terms, 'we have the right and the obligation to be men [sic] before God'.[31] To put this in non-gendered language: we are people, and remain people, albeit as individuals and in a world that is under judgement. To pick up Bonhoeffer's words again: '[Jesus] neither renders the human reality independent nor destroys it'.[32] We live under the sign of the cross where we *continue* to live and are witness to the in-breaking of the resurrection into earthly life. While I would take issue with Bonhoeffer's claim that this in-breaking is 'with every greater power into the earthly life', I can concur with what we have already seen from Moltmann, about that resurrection life 'win[ning] space for itself within it'.[33] What Bonhoeffer can then conclude is that, 'Christian life is participation in the encounter of Christ with the world', and that if the ultimate is to retain the space into which it in-breaks, then the penultimate must be preserved.[34] The biblical theme to which Bonhoeffer usefully turns here is the

---

29 Bonhoeffer, *Ethics*, p. 87.
30 Bonhoeffer, *Ethics*, p. 89.
31 Bonhoeffer, *Ethics*, p. 89.
32 Bonhoeffer, *Ethics*, p. 90.
33 Bonhoeffer, *Ethics*, p. 91.
34 Bonhoeffer, *Ethics*, p. 92.

familiar refrain, 'Prepare ye the way of the Lord, make his paths straight' (Luke 3.4), but without turning that injunction into a merely interior process.

This has immediate relevance for the concerns of critical discipleship and the challenge to neoliberal capitalist and imperial systems. Bonhoeffer knows full well that the penultimate affects how people perceive the ultimate; that God's grace is not an excuse for leaving people in misery:

> The state in which grace finds us is not a matter of indifference, even though it is always by grace alone that grace comes to us ... For him who is cast into utter shame, desolation, poverty and helplessness, it is difficult to have faith in the justice and goodness of God.[35]

When Bonhoeffer then goes on to make much of also preaching the word of grace, I begin to part company with him – at least in terms of what I perceive to be an unnecessary bifurcation of proclamation and demonstration. It is difficult to ensure that steps to preserve the penultimate do not degenerate into making the penultimate merely an instrument for effective preaching. This would instrumentalize rather than dignify the penultimate. The key here seems to me to be our participation in Christ's encounter with people-in-this-world. To put it less clumsily, we participate in Christ's encounter with embodied people; people whose bodies are sites of injustice, marginalization, poverty and disease – just as other bodies are sites of justice, incorporation and flourishing.

Does Bonhoeffer's position rule out our use of a term such as 'radical'? I think not, but it is a reclaimed radicalness that is self-reflexive in preparing the way – not simply for a more just world, but for Christ's encounter with the people of this world. That Christ is, if we think of him in the Gospels, radical in this sense too – but perhaps also subversive, another problematic term for critical discipleship and Practical Theology.

---

35 Bonhoeffer, *Ethics*, p. 94.

The seditious and subversive Christ

In what for many will be a surprising, even shocking, comparison, Mark Johnson has recently developed the notion of seditious theology by placing the punk movement of 1970s Britain alongside the biblical presentation of Jesus. Johnson finds that both Jesus and 1970s punks attempt 'imaginative re-identification' of the symbols currently drawn upon by their community. In Jesus' case, Johnson is interested in how he changed the values that were contained within symbols such as the land, the family, the Sabbath, and food – particularly in purity laws. Jesus uses *negation* as a rhetorical device. *All* possessions (without excluding the land) 'were now to be treated as nothing compared to the worth of his incoming kingdom'.[36] If we think that the British state has emotional and cultural, as well as strategic and economic, investment in territories such as Gibraltar and the Falkland Islands/Islas Malvinas, then we are but still only a fraction towards appreciating the Jews' view of The Land. For Jesus to relativize it in the light of his incoming kingdom is, as Johnson rightly observes, nothing short of sedition. Jesus also deploys *reversal* or 'scriptural *detournement*' – that is, 'the ability to take something being used to oppress and both expose those who so use it while liberating its meaning'.[37] Words and images, such as divorce, are turned to confront people.

Negation and reversal are further intensified by confrontation that included remarks against Pharisees, among others, that seemed aimed at stunning people. As Johnson puts it, Jesus 'had a clear aim in mind and arrested his listeners' thought processes and disrupted the way in which they received what he was saying, employing ... a sort of "imaginative" shock'.[38] We ought not, however, limit our appreciation of Jesus' seditious behaviour to confrontation, and Johnson helpfully presents the challenging inclusion that Jesus practised and advocated. Jesus was willing to engage – scandalously, it appears, in the eyes of many of his observers – with women

---

36 Mark Johnson, *Seditious Theology: Punk and the Ministry of Jesus*, Farnham: Ashgate, 2014, p. 102.
37 Johnson, *Seditious*, p. 108.
38 Johnson, *Seditious*, p. 119.

and outcasts. His call for love of enemies and his use of one as a symbol of righteous loving action (the Good Samaritan) is perhaps so familiar to us that we lose the radical, jolting effect that it seems to have been intended to evoke in his hearers. It is such a losing sight on the part of the Church of 'the seditious complexion' of Jesus that Johnson reflects upon.[39]

The depth to which any such loss has plumbed is not quantifiable nor is it uniform. It takes one form in the charismatic–evangelical traditions (the target of Johnson's particular criticism),[40] but will manifest itself differently in, for example, traditional European Roman Catholic popular piety. The difficulty within his generalizing 'the Church' as a social structure notwithstanding, Johnson is correct in locating at least the principal factors contributing to the loss of the seditious complexion of Jesus. These are the ways that the cross, itself a device of cruellest torture, has been represented in art and made so commonplace in Western culture that the audience (all people, including Christians) have become anaesthetized to it.[41]

Johnson's proposal for recovering not only the seditious tones of the cross, but of Jesus' ministry as a whole, are limited:

> By more consciously adopting the position of outsider, the church could, in part, rediscover its original place of marginalization and thereby help inoculate itself against the process of absorption. The pattern of sedition we have seen evidenced in our re-imaginings needs to remain as a 'poison' to that which surrounds it if the church is to increase its recovering of the seditious pattern of the words and work of Christ.[42]

Jesus talked about his followers being 'salt' and 'light', but here Johnson offers us the notion of 'poison'. Johnson had earlier in his text been a little more specific about this 'poison'. He draws on Westhelle's metaphor of allopathic cures which are effected

---

39 Johnson, *Seditious*, p. 149.
40 Johnson, *Seditious*, p. 151.
41 Johnson, *Seditious*, pp. 156–9.
42 Johnson, *Seditious*, p. 186.

by causing the body to react with effects that are harmful to the organism being tackled.[43] Johnson argues that subcultures (in his discussion of punk) are reflexive in the sense that they mirror back to society aspects of the wider culture that people would rather not face. What Johnson describes as 'a form of homeopathic poison' takes concrete form in the Church, being 'subversive, confrontational, paradoxical, anarchic, opposite, seditious and seen to be overturning that which, from the perspective of the kingdom, is in need of re-righting'.[44] The allusion here is to ultra-high dilutions of a substance that is delivered in a homeopathic treatment. Interestingly, the Homeopathic Society describes the aim to be 'triggering the body's natural system of healing'.[45] Now I do not want to unfairly push Johnson's metaphor into an allegory. But, setting aside the lack of widely accepted scientific evidence as to the effectiveness of homeopathy, the same could be said of the outcome of much (although not all) of the Church's work; it is an intriguing metaphor. It would need to be differentiated from an inoculation, lest the seditious activity of Christians prevent social change. However, if we believe with, for example, Moltmann (and perhaps with Bonhoeffer) that resurrection life may break into history then perhaps an allusion to the triggering of the body's natural system of healing is not too far awry after all.

'Poison' is a highly evocative and controversial metaphor for Christian witness and, coupled with notions of 'radicalization', becomes dangerously close to being a licence for extremism that damages people, infrastructure or property. Such violence is not in any way sanctioned by Johnson's proposals and, to repeat myself, is anathema to critical discipleship as I am formulating it.

Peter Neumann outlines the fault lines in conceptualizing radicalization. It is understood in terms of extremist beliefs ('cognitive radicalization') or extremist behaviour ('behavioural

---

43 Johnson, *Seditious*, p. 179. The reference is to Vitor Westhelle, *The Scandalous God: The Use and Abuse of the Cross*, Minneapolis, MN: Fortress Press, 2006.

44 Johnson, *Seditious*, pp. 181, 80.

45 http://www.homeopathy-soh.org/about-homeopathy/what-is-homeopathy/.

radicalization').[46] What is particularly ambiguous is the meaning of 'extremism'. On the one hand, it could be political ideas such as racial or religious supremacy, the denial of basic human rights or the disavowal of democracy. On the other hand, extremism can be defined by looking at the espoused methods, including physical violence and intimidation, kidnapping or wanton destruction of lives and property. Here, the political aims to which the extremist methods are directed are not, by analysts, foregrounded; it could be *any* political aim.[47]

The important point that Neumann makes is to challenge the assumption of organizations (such as the US Department of Homeland Security) that cognitive extremism comes first, then a person goes into action using extremist means. Researchers are concluding that extremist beliefs are but *one* of a number of routes or pathways that result in extremist action.[48]

To be a radical is not necessarily to be guilty of any crime, nor ought radicalism to be viewed as a problem to be solved. Neumann writes about the Revolutionary Wars of Independence by which the USA was founded: 'American history books are full of reminders that many of the rights and freedoms now taken for granted were fought for by individuals who were condemned as dangerous "radicals" by their contemporaries.'[49] Among more contemporary reminders are, as Neumann also points out, reactions by liberals to counter-terrorism legislation that is perceived as political moves against free speech that, without violent intent, otherwise upsets the status quo. We can see similar themes played out within churches – at local, national or international levels.

Christian institutions do not really like radicals – for reasons of vested interest and privilege that are akin to what we saw earlier around professional guilds. Radicals upset people and even commit what is now the secular 'unforgiveable sin' of causing offence. Radicals slow down decision-making processes – especially when

---

46 Peter R. Neumann, 'The Trouble with Radicalization', *International Affairs* 89.4 (2013), p. 873.
47 Neumann, 'The Trouble with Radicalization', following Scruton.
48 Neumann, 'The Trouble with Radicalization', p. 876.
49 Neumann, 'The Trouble with Radicalization', p. 877.

they plead the case of the voiceless whom it was otherwise rather easy to forget or perhaps silence. However, taking upon oneself the mantle of radical is no excuse for contrariness or feud-driven obstructionism. Clergy and lay people alike are not immune from such a temptation. Similarly, giving a limited hearing to – or appointing a token few – radicals may give the impression that an institution is progressive, but is a trap to which seasoned campaigners are quite alert.

Jesus was clearly assaulting the imagination of his audiences. In our terms he would be guilty of 'causing offence'. A line needs to be drawn between 'being offended' and 'being harmed' or threatened with harm. This distinction lies at the root of prohibitions against incitement to hatred and legitimate freedom of critical speech. To be offended is part of living in a society where different views are held and expressed. To incite or threaten harm is another matter altogether.[50]

Practical Theology as liberative ethics

The world is sadly rather familiar with radical, even offensive, Christians who contend for 'family values' or 'traditional ways of life' that are socially (and often also economically) conservative. The Practical Theology and critical discipleship I am advancing might hope to be as enthusiastic, but aiming towards a very different agenda. Miguel A. De La Torre, a Cuban Christian social ethicist teaching at Iliff School of Theology in Denver, CO, proposes 'liberative ethics' as 'a form of Practical Theology'.[51] His approach offers us a way of envisaging what a radicalized Practical Theology, that takes postcolonial critiques of Empire seriously, might look like.

---

50 For a broader discussion, see Eric Stoddart, 'Restrictions on the Gospel: Some Illegitimate Concerns of Evangelicals', *Modern Believing* 49.1 (2008), pp. 4–15.
51 De La Torre, 'Ethics', p. 342.

Against Eurocentric 'objective' deduction

'Liberative ethics', for De La Torre, 'is a spiritual response to un-examined normative and legitimized social structures responsible for privileging a powerful minority at the expense of the disenfran-chised majority'.[52] This model of ethics sees itself in opposition to the prevailing method that uses hypothetical cases from which *actual* experience is excluded, because bringing one's own or others' raw encounters with injustice (and in fact all aspects of life) makes the ethical reasoning too subjective.[53] A Eurocentric method teaches ethics as theories applied to cases in a deductive process that begins with a truth claim (usually, in Christian ethics, from the Bible or theological tradition) from which action is then deter-mined: 'ethics proceeds from doctrine'.[54]

De La Torre is also highly critical of Christian virtue ethics, exem-plified by Stanley Hauerwas, because it privileges the community's story of Christ with which Christians are to live consistently. That seems to be rather a non-contentious claim on the part of virtue ethicists – surely no one could disagree that Christians should make ethical decisions that are consistent with the Christian trad-ition? But, says De La Torre, this is to:

> confuse an unapologetic conviction about the truth of the Christian narrative with a Eurocentric interpretation of what that truth might be, thus converting [particular] truth claims into a façade masking a power that reinforces Eurocentric Christian dominance in ethics as well as in the culture.[55]

For De La Torre, such an approach means that Christians can get involved in – and in some forms of virtue ethics, even avoid – projects that are aimed at *dismantling* oppressive structures in society. The problem is particularly egregious when virtues are

52 Miguel A. De La Torre, 'Introduction', in Miguel A. De La Torre (ed.), *Ethics: A Liberative Approach*, Minneapolis, MN: Fortress Press, 2013, p. 3.
53 De La Torre, 'Ethics', p. 337.
54 De La Torre, 'Ethics', p. 338.
55 De La Torre, 'Ethics', p. 338.

based on rights because these are typically the rights 'that sustain the dominant culture'.[56] The main issue is that rights and virtue language has marginalized considerable sectors of the population (often the majority poor). Little, if any, regard is given to how social location actually informs ethical practice. As a result, given the privileged status of ethicists in the academy and Euro-American social systems, '*Eurocentric ethics* runs the danger of becoming indistinguishable from middle class respectability and conformity.'[57] Making 'objectivity' integral results in the person, group or culture engaging in ethic reasoning masking their subjectivity – perhaps as much to themselves as to the marginalized people who bear the brunt of decisions that maintain the privilege of those at the centre.

Susanne Johnson showed us how justice has dominated love. De La Torre argues similarly that law and order trump justice by Eurocentric ethicists who seek to preserve social order 'and their place within that society'.[58] De La Torre believes that an analysis of power relationships is missing – not only regarding the economic and political structures in which ethical decisions are implemented, but of Eurocentric ethics itself as a product of power.[59]

Liberative ethics are not necessarily Christian-based and so are differentiated from the more exclusively Christian Liberation Theology to which they are otherwise very close.[60] What is key is a commitment to ethics that aims at 'overturning structures of oppression'.[61] This is vigorously opposed to Eurocentric approaches that

---

56 De La Torre, 'Ethics', p. 338. De La Torre's example is the privileging of property rights over human rights so that someone who is starving is not allowed to take even a fallen apple from a tree belonging to a householder. Property rights – for the sake of public order and vested interests – prevail.

57 De La Torre, 'Ethics', p. 339.

58 De La Torre, 'Ethics', p. 341.

59 De La Torre, 'Ethics', p. 341. These concerns are very close to a feminist ethics of care – but liberative ethics gives particular attention to groups marginalized – largely but not exclusively – through race.

60 The possibilities of practical theological research that is in partnership with other faith groups have yet to be explored. It is one of my own long-term goals to take this path to examine how religious groups are affected by, and deploy, surveillance technologies and strategies.

61 De La Torre, 'Ethics', p. 342.

contribute – even when engaging in questions of social justice – to 'pacify[ing] the victims of social structures'.[62] Instead of hypothetical case studies liberative ethicists 'look to the daily existence of the world's wretched to wrestle with the ethical actions that should be taken in the messiness of life'.[63] Grounding case studies in everyday reality requires 'solidarity with one's marginalized community'.[64]

Liberative ethics and shared praxis

De La Torre's model of liberative ethics has considerable affinity to Groome's *Shared Praxis* which has featured heavily in our discussions. Liberative ethics begins with *observation* (similar to Groome's *naming*) in which we 'attempt to "see" through the eye of those who are made poor, victimized, and made to suffer'.[65] Here De La Torre is foregrounding a particular way of naming experience. This is not designed to be another attempt by the privileged to 'see for' or 'speak for' marginalized people with whom they do not share the same experience. It does mean, however, acknowledging the possibility of multiple marginalization. There is no 'neat dichotomy between "them", the dominant culture, and "us", the marginalized'.[66] Being a Cuban academic living in Colorado, De La Torre knows full well that he is simultaneously privileged and marginalized; his hyphenated status as Latino-American is significant.

In British Practical Theology – especially as it becomes more accessible to lay people – there will be some hyphenated identities, although proportionately fewer than in a country like the USA. Nevertheless, it will be important to take special care to enable people to name/observe their experience where parts of identity are marginalized.

After observation in De La Torre's model he has a focus on *reflection*, what Groome and others call *social analysis*. Here, it is

---

62 Miguel A. De La Torre, *Liberating Jonah: Forming an Ethics of Reconciliation*, Maryknoll, NY: Orbis Books, 2007, p. 90.

63 De La Torre, 'Ethics', p. 342.

64 De La Torre, 'Ethics', p. 343.

65 De La Torre, 'Ethics', p. 344.

66 De La Torre, 'Introduction', p. 2.

a case of paying particular attention to the social mechanisms that institutionalize oppression. The third step in the cycle of liberative ethics is *prayer* which is 'an attempt to understand the responsibility of communities of faith' not only as individuals but communally.[67] *Koinonia* is communion in solidarity, hearing stories of being marginalized and commitment to liberation. This bears considerable similarity to Groome's invitation to ask ourselves how we have been changed by hearing others' stories. The step De La Torre calls prayer will involve, for Christians, 'critical application of the biblical text to ... moral dilemmas' but, for other faiths and philosophies, would mean engagement with their respective scriptures and honoured traditions.[68] In Groome's and all cycles of practical theological reflection the same step is taken to critically appropriate biblical materials. A fourth step of *action* is that in which the preference of Eurocentric ethicists to theorize is supplanted by responses that aim at 'dismantling the presiding social structures that are detrimental to marginalized communities'.[69] Because *reflection* generates insights from social analysis that are brought into the following step, *prayer*, the step of putting social analysis and the Christian story into mutual critical engagement is not a distinct one in De La Torre's model. I think this is understandable if we recall that those doing liberative ethics will be those who have found the biblical and theological traditions to have contributed to their marginalization. The balance is tipped significantly towards seeing the colonialist, imperial or otherwise Eurocentric readings of the Bible as in need of substantial subversive – we might even say seditious – re-appropriation.

A fifth step for De La Torre has to be one of *reassessment*, making sure that the action undertaken is 'faithful to the message of liberation and salvation'.[70] In keeping with the vital insight of Freire, De La Torre is clear that the liberation is not only for the oppressed, but for the oppressors too: '[t]he hope of radically subverting and bringing about change in the way our political and economic

---

67 De La Torre, 'Ethics', p. 344.
68 De La Torre, 'Ethics', p. 344.
69 De La Torre, 'Ethics', p. 344.
70 De La Torre, 'Ethics', p. 345.

structures are constructed lies with the liberation of those complicit with the structure of oppression'.[71]

Reinforcing against central control

Liberative ethics is, I agree, a form of Practical Theology and one that coheres exceptionally well with the laicized, radicalized approach that I am advancing in this book. While Groome's (and in fact most models of Practical Theology) can accommodate the postcolonial emphasis of De La Torre's liberative ethics, they do not necessarily foreground it, nor with such a radical attention to challenging (with a view to dismantling) social structures of oppression. With models of theological action research coming to prominence in conjunction with a turn by many to ethnography and ecclesiology, the radical dimensions need careful reinforcement.

Elaine Graham has raised this very question in her critique of participatory action research in its theological clothing. Graham asks if

> action research and Practical Theology [are] simply aiming at improvement in practice, such as enhanced competence or strategic change? Or do they reflect a more radical epistemology that sees 'practice' as disclosive of meaning, and an understanding of action as a legitimate source of knowledge about the world – and in the case of Practical Theology, about God in the world?[72]

Action research starts with a problem, involves an action–reflection cycle, and is a collaborative process between insiders and, if necessary, some outside research experts. The outcomes are very much directed towards better technical competence and organizational change, but are also intent on facilitating people to internalize skills in exploring, reflecting and strategic planning. Graham correctly attributes John Swinton and Harriet Mowat with first bringing

---

71 De La Torre, *Liberating Jonah*, p. 77.

72 Elaine Graham, 'Is Practical Theology a Form of "Action Research"?', *International Journal of Practical Theology* 17.1 (2013), p. 149.

action research to prominence in Practical Theology in 2006.[73] Graham is also right to observe 'a degree of ambivalence' in Swinton and Mowat 'over the capacity of practice to reshape received tradition'.[74] God's revelation, in Christ, available in the Scriptures gives priority to theology. Graham concludes that Swinton and Mowat leave no space for practice and experience to be revelatory.[75] Graham also considers the more recent form of action research that is presented by the Action Research: Church and Society (ARCS) team, but finds that it does not do justice to 'the radical impact of first person action research'.[76] Graham offers the term *attentiveness* as a way of foregrounding the interconnection between the pursuit of change (in an organization or section of society) and the internalizing of skills that involves 'listening to the voices of disclosure and divine encounter'.[77] At its best, first person action research

---

73 John Swinton and Harriett Mowat, *Practical Theology and Qualitative Research*, London: SCM Press, 2006.

74 Graham, 'Is Practical Theology', p. 160.

75 Graham, 'Is Practical Theology', p. 160. Swinton and Mowat do pretty much nail their theological colours to the mast with, as Graham reminds us, a statement like, '[e]xperience and human reason cannot lead us ... to an understanding of the cross and the resurrection' (Swinton and Mowat, *Practical Theology*, p. 5). The debate around the control of ethnography (and indeed any form of empirical research) by dogmatic theology is visible very clearly in John Webster, '"In the Society of God": Some Principles of Ecclesiology', in Pete Ward (ed.), *Perspectives on Ecclesiology and Ethnography*, Grand Rapids, MI; Cambridge, UK: Eerdmans, 2012, pp. 200–22. A response has been offered: see Christopher Craig Brittain, 'Why Ecclesiology Cannot Live by Doctrine Alone: A Reply to John Webster's "in the Society of God"', *Ecclesial Practices* 1 (2014), pp. 5–30. Brittain's defence of the contribution of ethnography to ecclesiology goes as far as 'discernment of the Spirit's activity', thereby 'nurturing corporate spiritual discernment' that can lead to a confession of failure (Brittain, 'Why Ecclesiology', pp. 28, 29). Any revision of doctrine by experience does not seem to be admissible; the possibility of God's revelatory actions beyond ecclesial practice is not discussed, but Brittain's stance would seem to me to imply this is not envisaged.

76 Helen Cameron *et al.*, *Talking About God in Practice: Theological Action Research and Practical Theology*, London: SCM Press, 2010; Graham, 'Is Practical Theology', p. 164.

77 Graham, 'Is Practical Theology', p. 170.

is about being in practice a more authentic person. Attending to the divine is an integral component of such an aim: '[u]ltimately ... the purpose of reflective inquiry such as action research is the flourishing of the human and more-than-human world, in all its complexity and interconnectedness'.[78]

Graham helps us see what can be at stake for a Practical Theology that aligns itself with liberative ethics. It will be a form of Practical Theology that gains increasing distance from models that reserve divine revelation to Scripture and exclude human experience. Privileging dogmatic theology by placing experience finally under its control is not acceptable to a postcolonialist critique that has known – and continues to live – marginalization at the hands of the central levers of power.

Seeing liberative ethics as a form of Practical Theology does not mean that we simply subsume Practical Theology into this approach to ethical decision-making. Practical Theology's tools – not only in empirical research but in sophisticated dialogue between social analysis and the Christian story – are vital dimensions of the liberative project. There also has to be a place for those of us who find ourselves in privileged contexts. I am not suggesting that we would be excluded from the community of liberative ethicists. Nor am I proposing that Practical Theology becomes a home for the bourgeois, while liberative ethics accommodates the subaltern. Any such bifurcation would be retrogressive.

What I am proposing is that the imagined community of Practical Theology submit itself to liberative ethics. Integral, then, to any cycle of reflection must be the voice, needs and contribution of those who are marginalized, disenfranchised or in other ways oppressed by Empire. This does not mean adding an extra step to the diagrams of the cycle of reflection, but radicalizing each step in order to disturb our critical discipleship.

---

78 Graham, 'Is Practical Theology', p. 172.

Coda
A Letter to 1996 from 2014

Dear Eric,

First things first, your flights home from Johannesburg will land safely so you can stop worrying.

You won't find many who will understand your fears of theological blind spots – at least not in the circles in which you're currently moving. But don't let that stop you seeking out writers who, unlike you, can't fly out of economic and theological marginalization. The windows that have opened up now you have begun to appreciate the power of people's own voice will let you look out on a landscape in which you will catch glimpses of resurrection life; it does not only lie over the horizon.

That PhD you're about to begin ... you'll complete it, and the God in whom you hope now (in your frustratingly pessimistic way) will turn out to be bigger and less dependent on Christians than you expect. That discovery will let you work your way through cynicism, then scepticism, to reach a way of being that you'll call critical discipleship but which others, who have been well ahead of you, know by different terms.

Don't surrender to those who expect you to be a *real* theologian; you can be proud to do theology that dares not speak its name. Your frustration at Church and clergy will be re-directed too. It will be a catalyst that sparks your interest in enabling ordinary people to do theology in their context.

(But don't give clergy too hard a time; you remember what it can be like, so don't project all your shortcomings on to those who persevere at the pastoral coalface.)

145

You will keep being astounded when the Practical Theology process works and people make connections and gain insight to their practice of faith.

You'll have the privilege of seeing that in students of all ages, and you'll be part of their stories for a little while, but rarely know how their critical take on their professional life works out in the long run. I know you don't do flamboyant outrage, but you will have a small role in disturbing a few Christians who would otherwise settle for poverty and injustice in their society as normal. There will be months, sometimes years, when becoming aware of so many perspectives will be disconcerting, to say the least. You are you, but don't be afraid to open yourself to others' narratives, beyond the point that it is comfortable for you.

There are Practical Theologians waiting to welcome you so listen to them; this community has a lot to teach you. Of all theologians, those chaplains who sit with the dying know that hardship cannot be wished away and that God's interventions are all too elusive; that faith is uncoupled from triumphalism. Let their stance against the power of death to encamp in life be a metaphor for you to resist, in your small ways, the totality of the Empire.

And no, Scotland will not be invaded by imperial forces; that's not what I mean. But it will not be easy for you to see how you are being shaped by economic forces, and you will need your wits about you when you find you're part of a nation and her allies at war in the Fertile Crescent.

Remember that very first sermon you preached in the Baptist Church – the one on the Beatitudes that you're already thinking about reprising at your final Sunday morning when you get back to Scotland? Those Beatitudes will come to be at the heart of your Practical Theology – but it's going to take a long time to recognize that.

Oh, and you'll end up as a lay Anglo-Catholic Scottish Episcopalian – bet you didn't see that coming!

With love from your future,

Eric

Bibliography

Aguilar, Mario, *The History and Politics of Latin American Theology – Volume 2*, London: SCM Press, 2008.

Anderson, Benedict, *Imagined Communities: New Edition*, London: Verso, 2006 [1983].

Anderson, Herbert, 'Seeing the Other Whole: A Habitus for Globalization', in Paul H. Ballard and Pamela D. Couture (eds), *Globalization and Difference: Practical Theology in a World Context*, Fairwater, Cardiff: Cardiff Academic Press, 1999, pp. 3–17.

Andolsen, Barbara Hilkert, 'Agape in Feminist Ethics', *Journal of Religious Ethics* 9.1 (1981), pp. 69–83.

Andrews, Dale P., 'West Africa', in Bonnie J. Miller-McLemore (ed.), *The Wiley-Blackwell Companion to Practical Theology*, Chichester: Wiley-Blackwell, 2012, pp. 401–11.

Aquino, Maria Pilar, 'Latina Feminist Theology: Central Features', in Maria Pilar Aquino *et al.* (eds), *A Reader in Latina Feminist Theology: Religion and Justice*, Austin, TX: University of Texas Press, 2002, pp. 133–60.

Arendt, Hannah, *The Human Condition*, second edn, Chicago: University of Chicago Press, 1998 [1958].

Barber, Christopher, 'On Connectedness: Spirituality on the Autistic Spectrum', *Practical Theology* 4.2 (2011), pp. 201–11.

Bass, Dorothy C., 'Eating', in Bonnie J. Miller-McLemore (ed.), *The Wiley-Blackwell Companion to Practical Theology*, Chichester: Wiley-Blackwell, 2012, pp. 51–60.

Bauman, Zygmunt, *Work, Consumerism and the New Poor*, Buckingham: Open University Press, 1990.

Baxter, Richard, *The Reformed Pastor*, London: SCM Press, 1956 [1656].

Berry, Jan, *Ritual Making Women: Shaping Rites for Changing Lives*, London: Equinox, 2009.

Bonhoeffer, Dietrich, *Ethics*, ed. Eberhard Bethge, London: SCM Press, 1955.

Bons-Storm, Riet, 'Thinking and Living Diversities in Practical Theology', in Paul H. Ballard and Pamela D. Couture (eds), *Globalization and Difference: Practical Theology in a World Context*, Fairwater, Cardiff: Cardiff Academic Press, 1999, pp. 123–7.

Bradley, Ian, *Believing in Britain: The Spiritual Identity of 'Britishness'*, London: I. B. Taurus, 2007.

Brandt, James M., 'Historical Theology', in Bonnie J. Miller-McLemore (ed.), *The Wiley-Blackwell Companion to Practical Theology*, Chichester: Wiley-Blackwell, 2012, pp. 367–76.

Brittain, Christopher Craig, 'Why Ecclesiology Cannot Live by Doctrine Alone: A Reply to John Webster's "in the Society of God"', *Ecclesial Practices* 1 (2014), pp. 5–30.

Brown, Michael Joseph, 'Biblical Theology', in Bonnie J. Miller-McLemore (ed.), *The Wiley-Blackwell Companion to Practical Theology*, Chichester: Wiley-Blackwell, 2012, pp. 377–85.

Brown, Sally A., 'Hermeneutical Theory', in Bonnie J. Miller-McLemore (ed.), *The Wiley-Blackwell Companion to Practical Theology*, Chichester: Wiley-Blackwell, 2012, pp. 112–22.

Browning, Don, 'Practical Theology and Political Theology', *Theology Today* 42.1 (1985), pp. 15–33.

Browning, Don, *A Fundamental Practical Theology: Descriptive and Strategic Proposals*, Minneapolis: Fortress Press, 1996.

Butler Jr, Lee H., 'Psychological Theory', in Bonnie J. Miller-McLemore (ed.), *The Wiley-Blackwell Companion to Practical Theology*, Chichester: Wiley-Blackwell, 2012, pp. 102–11.

Cahalan, Kathleen A., 'Integration in Theological Education', in Bonnie J. Miller-McLemore (ed.), *The Wiley-Blackwell Companion to Practical Theology*, Chichester: Wiley-Blackwell, 2012, pp. 386–95.

Cameron, Helen *et al.*, *Talking About God in Practice: Theological Action Research and Practical Theology*, London: SCM Press, 2010.

Campbell, Alistair V., *Rediscovering Pastoral Care*, London: Darton, Longman & Todd, 1981.

Campbell, Alistair V., *Paid to Care? The Limits of Professionalism in Pastoral Care*, London: SPCK, 1985.

Chopp, Rebecca S., 'Practical Theology and Liberation', in Lewis S. Mudge and James N. Poling (eds), *Formation and Reflection: The Promise of Practical Theology*, Philadelphia: Fortress Press, 1987, pp. 120–38.

Clayton, Mark, 'Contemplative Chaplaincy? A View from a Children's Hospice', *Practical Theology* 6.1 (2013), pp. 35–50.

Connolly, Hugh, *The Irish Penitentials and Their Significance for the Sacrament of Penance Today*, Blackrock, County Dublin: Four Courts Press, 1995.

Cooper-White, Pamela, 'Suffering', in Bonnie J. Miller-McLemore (ed.), *The Wiley-Blackwell Companion to Practical Theology*, Chichester: Wiley-Blackwell, 2012, pp. 23–31.

Couture, Pamela D., 'Social Policy', in Bonnie J. Miller-McLemore (ed.), *The Wiley-Blackwell Companion to Practical Theology*, Chichester: Wiley-Blackwell, 2012, pp. 153–62.

D'Arcy, Martin C., *The Mind and Heart of Love*, London: Faber & Faber, 1946.

Dahill, Lisa E., *Reading from the Underside of Selfhood: Bonhoeffer and Spiritual Formation*, Eugene, OR: Pickwick Publications, 2009.

De La Torre, Miguel A., *Liberating Jonah: Forming an Ethics of Reconciliation*, Maryknoll, NY: Orbis Books, 2007.

De La Torre, Miguel A., 'Ethics', in Bonnie J. Miller-McLemore (ed.), *The Wiley-Blackwell Companion to Practical Theology*, Chichester: Wiley-Blackwell, 2012, pp. 337–46.

De La Torre, Miguel A., 'Introduction', in *Ethics: A Liberative Approach*, Minneapolis, MN: Fortress Press, 2013, pp. 1–6.

De La Torre, Miguel A., and Albert Hernández, *The Quest for the Historical Satan*, Minneapolis, MN: Fortress Press, 2011.

Devine, T. M., *The Scottish Nation 1700–2000*, London: Penguin Books, 1999.

Dewey, John, *Experience and Nature*, London: Open Court, 1958 [1925].

Dube, Musa W., *Postcolonial Feminist Interpretation of the Bible*, St Louis, MI: Chalice Press, 2000.

Dunlop, Susan J., 'Healing', in Bonnie J. Miller-McLemore (ed.), *The Wiley-Blackwell Companion to Practical Theology*, Chichester: Wiley-Blackwell, 2012, pp. 32–41.

Dykstra, Craig, *Vision and Character: A Christian Educator's Alternative to Kohlberg*, New York: Paulist Press, 1981.

Erik and Vicki Johnson, 'Pastor's Bad Day', Leadership Journal, http://www.christianitytoday.com/le/2004/may-online-only/pastors-bad-day.html.

Evetts, Julia *et al.*, 'Professionalization, Scientific Expertise, and Elitism: A Sociological Perspective', in K. Anders Ericsson *et al.* (eds), *The Cambridge Handbook of Expertise and Expert Performance*, Cambridge: Cambridge University Press, 2006, pp. 105–23.

Foucault, Michel, *Discipline and Punish: The Birth of the Prison*, London: Penguin Books, 1977.

Foucault, Michel, 'The Ethics of the Concern for Self as a Practice of Freedom', in *Michel Foucault, Ethics: Subjectivity and Truth. The Essential Works of Foucault 1954–1984, Vol. 1*, ed. R. Rabinow, London: Penguin Books, 2000, pp. 281–301.

Freire, Paulo, *Pedagogy of the Oppressed*, London: Penguin Books, 1970.

Ganzevoort, R. Ruard, 'Narrative Approaches', in Bonnie J. Miller-McLemore (ed.), *The Wiley-Blackwell Companion to Practical Theology*, Chichester: Wiley-Blackwell, 2012, pp. 214–23.

Gay, Doug, *Honey from the Lion: Christianity and the Ethics of Nationalism*, London: SCM Press, 2013.

Geertz, Clifford, *The Interpretation of Cultures: Selected Essays*, London: Fontana, 1993 (1973).

Graham, Elaine, *Transforming Practice: Pastoral Theology in an Age of Uncertainty*, London: Mowbray, 1996.

Graham, Elaine, 'Feminist Theory', in Bonnie J. Miller-McLemore (ed.), *The Wiley-Blackwell Companion to Practical Theology*, Chichester: Wiley-Blackwell, 2012, pp. 193–203.

Graham, Elaine, 'Is Practical Theology a Form of "Action Research"?', *International Journal of Practical Theology* 17.1 (2013), pp. 148–78.

Graham, Elaine, and Margaret Halsey (eds), *Life Cycles: Women and Pastoral Care*, London: SPCK, 1993.

Graham, Elaine *et al.*, *Theological Reflection: Methods*, London: SCM Press, 2005.

Greider, Kathleen J., 'Religious Pluralism and Christian-Centrism', in Bonnie J. Miller-McLemore (ed.), *The Wiley-Blackwell Companion to Practical Theology*, Chichester: Wiley-Blackwell, 2012, pp. 452–62.

Grey, Mary C., 'Feminist Images of Redemption in Education', *British Journal of Religious Education* 12.1 (1989), pp. 20–8.

Groome, Thomas H., 'Theology on Our Feet: A Revisionist Pedagogy for Healing the Gap between Academia and Ecclesia', in Lewis S. Mudge and James N. Poling (eds), *Formation and Reflection: The Promise of Practical Theology*, Philadelphia: Fortress Press, 1987, pp. 55–78.

Groome, Thomas H., 'Religious Knowing: Still Looking for That Tree', *Religious Education* 92.2 (1997), pp. 204–26.

Groome, Thomas H., *Sharing Faith: A Comprehensive Approach to Religious Education and Pastoral Ministry: The Way of Shared Praxis*, Eugene, OR: Wipf and Stock, 1998.

Gutiérrez, Gustavo, *Praxis De Liberacion Y Fe Cristianan*, Madrid: Zero, 1974.

Gutiérrez, Gustavo, *We Drink from Our Own Wells*, London: SCM Press, 2005.

Gutiérrez, Gustavo, *A Theology of Liberation*, London: SCM Press, 2001 [1974].

Hahn, Meerha, 'South Korea', in Bonnie J. Miller-McLemore (ed.), *The Wiley-Blackwell Companion to Practical Theology*, Chichester: Wiley-Blackwell, 2012, pp. 534–43.

Hampson, Daphne, *Swallowing a Fishbone?: Feminist Theologians Debate Christianity*, London: SPCK, 1996.

Hauerwas, Stanley, *The Peaceable Kingdom: A Primer in Christian Ethics*, London: SCM Press, 1984.

Hess, Carol Lakey, 'Religious Education', in Bonnie J. Miller-McLemore (ed.), *The Wiley-Blackwell Companion to Practical Theology*, Chichester: Wiley-Blackwell, 2012, pp. 299–307.

Ipsos MORI, *Perils of Perception*, London: Royal Statistical Society, King's College London and Ipsos MORI, 2013.

Jinkins, Michael, 'Religious Leadership', in Bonnie J. Miller-McLemore (ed.), *The Wiley-Blackwell Companion to Practical Theology*, Chichester: Wiley-Blackwell, 2012, pp. 308–17.

Joas, Hans, *The Creativity of Action*, trans. by Jeremy Gaines and Paul Keast, Cambridge: Polity Press, 1996.

Joas, Hans, 'Action Is the Way in Which Humans Beings Exist in the World – Interview', Dialog On Leadership, http://www.iwp.jku.at/born/mpwfst/02/www.dialogonleadership.org/Joasx1999.html#nine.

Joas, Hans, and Jens Beckert, 'Action Theory', in J. H. Turner (ed.), *Handbook of Sociological Theory*, New York: Kluwer Academic/Plenum Publishers, 2001, pp. 269–85.

Johnson, Mark, *Seditious Theology: Punk and the Ministry of Jesus*, Farnham: Ashgate, 2014.

Johnson, Susanne, 'Remembering the Poor: Transforming Christian Practice', in Dana R. Wright and John D. Kuentzel (eds), *Redemptive Transformation in Practical Theology: Essays in Honor of James E. Loder Jr.*, Grand Rapids, MI, and Cambridge, UK: William B. Eerdmans, 2004, pp. 189–215.

Jolly, Ruth Ann, 'Chaplaincy Works', *Practical Theology* 4.3 (2011), pp. 359–61.

Kendrick, Graham, 'Let God Arise', Kingsway Music Ltd, 1984.

Kim, Sebastian, *Theology in the Public Sphere: Public Theology as Catalyst for Open Debate*, London: SCM Press, 2011.

Kwok Pui-lan, 'Making the Connections: Postcolonial Studies and Feminist Biblical Interpretation', in R. S. Sugirtharajah (ed.), *The Postcolonial Biblical Reader*, Oxford: Blackwell, 2006, pp. 45–63.

Lartey, Emmanuel, 'Practical Theology as a Theological Form', in James Woodward and Stephen Pattison (eds), *The Blackwell Reader in Pastoral and Practical Theology*, Oxford: Blackwell, 2000 [1996], pp. 128–34.

Lester, Andrew D., *Hope in Pastoral Care and Counseling*, Louisville, KY: Westminster John Knox, 1995.

Long, Anne, *Listening*, Daybreak, 1990.

Mager, Robert, 'Do We Learn to Know God from What We Do? A Plea for a Relational Concept of Action', in Elaine Graham and Anna Rowlands (eds), *Pathways to the Public Square*, Münster: Lit Verlag, 2005, pp. 191–201.

Mager, Robert, 'Action Theories', in Bonnie J. Miller-McLemore (ed.), *The Wiley-Blackwell Companion to Practical Theology*, Chichester: Wiley-Blackwell, 2012, pp. 255–65.

Maxwell-Stuart, P. G., *Satan: A Biography*, Stroud: Amberley Publishing, 2008.

Mejido, Manuel, 'Beyond the Postmodern Condition, or the Turn toward Psychoanalysis', in Ivan Petrella (ed.), *Latin American Liberation Theology: The Next Generation*, Maryknoll, NY: Orbis Books, 2005, pp. 119–46.

Mercer, Joyce Ann, 'Economics, Class, and Classism', in Bonnie J. Miller-McLemore (ed.), *The Wiley-Blackwell Companion to Practical Theology*, Chichester: Wiley-Blackwell, 2012, pp. 432–42.

Metz, Johannes Baptist, *Faith in History and Society: Toward a Practical Fundamental Theology*, trans. by David Smith, New York: Seabury Press, 1980.

Metz, Johannes Baptist, *The Emergent Church: The Future of Christianity in a Post-Bourgeois World*, trans. by Peter Mann, New York: Crossroad, 1981.

Míguez, Néstor *et al.*, *Beyond the Spirit of Empire: Theology and Politics in a New Key*, London: SCM Press, 2009.

Miller-McLemore, Bonnie J., 'Introduction: The Contributions of Practical Theology', in Bonnie J. Miller-McLemore (ed.), *The Wiley-Blackwell Companion to Practical Theology*, Chichester: Wiley-Blackwell, 2012, pp. 1–20.

Miller-McLemore, Bonnie J., *The Wiley-Blackwell Companion to Practical Theology*, Chichester: Wiley-Blackwell, 2012.

Moen, Don, *Worship with Don Moen*, Integrity Hosanna Music, 1992.

Moltmann, Jürgen, *Theology of Hope: On the Ground and the Implications of a Christian Eschatology*, London: SCM Press, 1967.

Moltmann, Jürgen, *The Crucified God*, London: SCM Press, 1974.

Moltmann, Jürgen, *The Trinity and the Kingdom of God*, London: SCM Press, 1981.

Murphy, R., *Social Closure: The Theory of Monopolization and Exclusion*, Oxford: Clarendon Press, 1988.

Nee, Watchman, *The Normal Christian Life*, London: Victory Press, 1963.

Nee, Watchman, *A Table in the Wilderness: Daily Meditations from the Ministry of Watchman Nee*, London: Victory Press, 1969.

Nelson, James B., 'Review: "The Moral Context of Pastoral Care" by Don Browning', *Journal of Religion* 60 (1980), pp. 111–13.

Neuger, Christie Cozad (ed.), *The Arts of Ministry: Feminist–Womanist Approaches*, Louisville: Westminster John Knox Press, 1996.

Neumann, Peter R., 'The Trouble with Radicalization', *International Affairs* 89.4 (2013), pp. 873–93.

Noddings, Nel, *Caring: A Feminine Approach to Ethics & Moral Education*, Berkeley and London: University of California Press, 1984.

Nouwen, Henri, *The Wounded Healer*, London: Darton, Longman & Todd, 1994.

Nwachuku, Daisy N., 'West Africa', in Bonnie J. Miller-McLemore (ed.), *The Wiley-Blackwell Companion to Practical Theology*, Chichester: Wiley-Blackwell, 2012, pp. 515–24.

Osmer, Richard R., 'The United States', in Bonnie J. Miller-McLemore (ed.), *The Wiley-Blackwell Companion to Practical Theology*, Chichester: Wiley-Blackwell, 2012, pp. 495–504.

Parker, Evelyn L., 'Womanist Theory', in Bonnie J. Miller-McLemore (ed.), *The Wiley-Blackwell Companion to Practical Theology*, Chichester: Wiley-Blackwell, 2012, pp. 204–13.

Pattison, Stephen, *A Critique of Pastoral Care*, London: SCM Press, 1988.

Pattison, Stephen, *Pastoral Care and Liberation Theology*, Cambridge: Cambridge University Press, 1994.

Petrella, Ivan, *The Future of Liberation Theology: An Argument and Manifesto*, London: SCM Press, 2006.

Petrella, Ivan, *Beyond Liberation Theology: A Polemic*, London: SCM Press, 2008.

Ramsay, Nancy J., 'Emancipatory Theory and Method', in Bonnie J. Miller-McLemore (ed.), *The Wiley-Blackwell Companion to Practical Theology*, Chichester: Wiley-Blackwell, 2012, pp. 183–92.

Reader, John, 'The Professionalisation of Voluntary Activity', *Contact* 144 (2004), pp. 14–22.

Reader, John, *Reconstructing Practical Theology: The Impact of Globalization*, Aldershot: Ashgate, 2008.

Richard, Pablo, 'Teología De La Solidaridad En El Contexto Actual De Economía Neoliberal De Mercado', in Franz Hinkelammert (ed.), *El Huracán De La Globalización*, San José, Coasta Rica: DEI, 1999, pp. 223–38.

Ringe, Sharon H., 'A Gentile Woman's Story', in Letty M. Russell (ed.), *Feminist Interpretation of the Bible*, Oxford: Blackwell, 1985, pp. 65–72.

Rogers, Carl R., *On Becoming a Person: A Therapist's View of Psychotherapy*, London: Constable & Co., 1961.

Rooms, Nigel, 'Paul as Practical Theologian: *Phronesis* in Philippians', *Practical Theology* 5.1 (2012), pp. 81–94.

Rowell, Geoffrey, *Hell and the Victorians*, Oxford: Clarendon Press, 1974.

Saliers, Don E., 'Worship', in Bonnie J. Miller-McLemore (ed.), *The Wiley-Blackwell Companion to Practical Theology*, Chichester: Wiley-Blackwell, 2012, pp. 289–98.

Savage, Mike *et al.*, 'A New Model of Social Class? Findings from the BBC's Great British Class Survey Experiment', *Sociology* 47.2 (2013), pp. 219–50.

Scalise, Charles J., 'Protestant Evangelicalism', in Bonnie J. Miller-McLemore (ed.), *The Wiley-Blackwell Companion to Practical Theology*, Chichester: Wiley-Blackwell, 2012, pp. 577–86.

Scharen, Christian, 'Blessing', in Bonnie J. Miller-McLemore (ed.), *The Wiley-Blackwell Companion to Practical Theology*, Chichester: Wiley-Blackwell, 2012, pp. 80–8.

Sharp, Melinda McGarrah, 'Globalization, Colonialism, and Postcolonialism', in Bonnie J. Miller-McLemore (ed.), *The Wiley-Blackwell Companion to Practical Theology*, Chichester: Wiley-Blackwell, 2012, pp. 422–31.

Shaw, Anna Howard, The Dillon Collection, the Shaw Series, The Dillon Collection, the Shaw Series, The Schlesinger Library, Radcliffe College.

Smith, Donald, *Freedom and Faith: A Question of Scottish Identity*, Edinburgh: St Andrew Press, 2013.

Sociedad, 'Sólo Le Pido Adios', http://edant.clarin.com/diario/2006/04/02/sociedad/s-01169625.htm.

Stoddart, Eric, 'Hell in Scotland: A Survey of Where the Nation's Clergy Think Some Might Be Heading', *Contact* 143 (2004), pp. 14–27.

Stoddart, Eric, 'Living Theology: A Methodology for Issues-Led Theological Reflection in Higher Education', *British Journal of Theological Education* 14.2 (2004), pp. 187–207.

Stoddart, Eric, 'Spirituality and Citizenship: Sacramentality in a Parable', *Theological Studies* 68 (2007), pp. 761–79.

Stoddart, Eric, 'Restrictions on the Gospel: Some Illegitimate Concerns of Evangelicals', *Modern Believing* 49.1 (2008), pp. 4–15.

Stoddart, Eric, *Theological Perspectives on a Surveillance Society: Watching and Being Watched*, Aldershot: Ashgate, 2011.

Stone, Ken, 'Border Anxiety: Food, Sex and the Boundaries of Identity', in *Practising Safer Texts: Food, Sex and Bible in Queer Perspective*, London: T. & T. Clark, 2005, pp. 46–67.

Streck, Valburga Schmiedt, 'Brazil', in Bonnie J. Miller-McLemore (ed.), *The Wiley-Blackwell Companion to Practical Theology*, Chichester: Wiley-Blackwell, 2012, pp. 525–33.

Stuart, Elizabeth, *Gay and Lesbian Theologies: Repetitions with Critical Difference*, Aldershot: Ashgate, 2003.

Sugirtharajah, R. S., *Postcolonial Reconfigurations: An Alternative Way of Reading the Bible and Doing Theology*, London: SCM Press, 2003.

Swinton, John, *Dementia: Living in the Memories of God*, London: SCM Press, 2012.

Swinton, John, 'Disability, Ableism, and Disablism', in Bonnie J. Miller-McLemore (ed.), *The Wiley-Blackwell Companion to Practical Theology*, Chichester: Wiley-Blackwell, 2012, pp. 443–51.

Swinton, John, and Harriet Mowat, *Practical Theology and Qualitative Research*, London: SCM Press, 2006.

Townes, Emilie M., 'Living in the New Jerusalem: The Rhetoric and Movement of Liberation in the House of Evil', in *A Troubling in My Soul: Womanist Perspectives on Evil and Suffering*, Markyknoll, NY: Orbis, 2002, pp. 78–91.

Tozer, A. W., *Knowledge of the Holy*, New York: Harper & Row, 1961.

Tracy, David, 'The Foundations of Practical Theology', in Don S. Browning (ed.), *Practical Theology: The Emerging Field in Theology, Church and World*, San Francisco: Harper & Row, 1983, pp. 61–82.

Turpin, Katherine, 'Consuming', in Bonnie J. Miller-McLemore (ed.), *The Wiley-Blackwell Companion to Practical Theology*, Chichester: Wiley-Blackwell, 2012, pp. 70–9.

Urquhart, Colin, *When the Spirit Comes*, London: Hodder & Stoughton, 1974.

Urquhart, Colin, *My Father Is the Gardener*, London: Hodder & Stoughton, 1977.

Various, 'Review: The Wiley-Blackwell Companion to Practical Theology', *Practical Theology* 7.1 (2014), pp. 63–73.

Walker, D. P., *The Decline of Hell: Seventeenth-Century Discussions of Eternal Treatment*, London: Routledge & Kegan Paul, 1964.

Walton, Heather, *Imagining Theology: Women, Writing, and God*, London: T. & T. Clark, 2007.

Walton, Heather, 'Poetics', in Bonnie J. Miller-McLemore (ed.), *The Wiley-Blackwell Companion to Practical Theology*, Chichester: Wiley-Blackwell, 2012, pp. 173–82.

Watson, David, *Discipleship*, London: Hodder & Stoughton, 1981.

Webster, John, '"In the Society of God": Some Principles of Ecclesiology', in Pete Ward (ed.), *Perspectives on Ecclesiology and Ethnography*, Grand Rapids, MI; Cambridge, UK: Eerdmans, 2012, pp. 200–22.

Westhelle, Vítor, *The Scandalous God: The Use and Abuse of the Cross*, Minneapolis, MN: Fortress Press, 2006.

Whitehead, James D., 'The Practical Play of Theology', in Lewis S. Mudge and James N. Poling (eds), *Formation and Reflection: The Promise of Practical Theology*, Philadelphia: Fortress Press, 1987, pp. 36–54.

Wilmore, Gayraud S., *Black Theology and Black Radicalism: An Interpretation of the Religious History of Afro-American People*, Maryknoll, NY: Orbis Books, 1983.

Wolfteich, Claire E., 'Spirituality', in Bonnie J. Miller-McLemore (ed.), *The Wiley-Blackwell Companion to Practical Theology*, Chichester: Wiley-Blackwell, 2012, pp. 328–36.

Woman's Claim of Right Group, *A Woman's Claim of Right in Scotland*, Edinburgh: Polygon, 1991.

Wright, Frank, *Pastoral Care Revisited*, London: SCM Press, 1996.

X, Malcolm, 'Speech at the Founding Rally of the Organization of Afro-American Unity, Given at Harlem 28th June 1964', in *By Any Means Necessary: Speeches, Interviews, and a Letter by Malcolm X*, New York: Pathfinder Press, 1970.

Index